"Y'got two left arms, an' yer wind's unsound,
Y'got two right legs that stick to the ground,
An' yer feet have been fixed on wrong way round!"

"You're cross eyed and knock-kneed, darn me."
"YOU'RE DEAF!" he says, "You stars and a blank,
You can't walk straight an' you can't keep rank.
You'd pass maybe for a shop or a bank,
But you ain't no good for the army!"

"Shoulder Arms! Form Fours! Quick March. Keep Pace.
Mark Time! Right Turn! Halt! YOU ******* DISGRACE!"
So he kept us at it all over the place,
Till the sweat rolled off us in streams.
Seems as he wanted to cure or to kill,
Nothin' all day but route marches an' drill.
An' all night long, if we slept we were still,
A formin' fours in our dreams.

Then at last he spoke as a Christian should:
"When they brought you to me you was lumps,
But now you are men, you are flesh an' blood,
You are real live soldiers, s'welp me!
An' if you're as square as you orter be,
When the Padre asks, 'Who made yer?' says he –
You'll tell him the truth an' say it was ME –
An' Gawd didn't even help me!"

There's several ways to wherever you go,
But there's only one way to the blokes that know.
They get there quickest by travellin' slow,
An' that's why they're worth their blunt.
I guess it's a howler, at any rate,
To be there too early, or there too late.
An' the Sergeant knew, an' was showin' us straight,
The shortest way to the front.

"Hen pecked and harried husbands... now Heroes".

"SONNY 10" – WALTER LEE OF THE ROYAL NAVAL DIVISION

While I was on night duty in Mary Ward, July 1915, a fresh case was admitted into Luke Ward.

Walter Lee aged 16, of the R.N.D. complained of a sore spot on the left heel when up at the Crystal Palace. No attention was paid to the same and after going on parade for three days in great pain, he was put in the sick bay. There he was left entirely to himself for 24 hours, until he finally fell out of his hammock! This alarmed those in authority and he was immediately sent to C.G.H. It was too late. Spite every effort his leg could not be saved, secondary haemorrhage occurring twice. Dr Adams preformed the operation of which I was present.

Sonny 10 was a great favourite with all and exceedingly plucky. He christened his stump "gollywog" and wished to pay for his wooden leg lest folk should say he was paid for *"doing his bit"*.

43 Martin Lane
Upperthorpe,
Sheffield

Nov 16th

Dear Nurse,

Just a few lines hoping to find you in the best of health as it leaves me at present. I'm sure it was very kind of you to write to me as you, nurse, have not much rest. I remember only too well the Sunday when you stayed at the hospital just to look after me. Am sure it was very kind of you to give up your Sunday's rest. How I miss dear old St. Luke. I sit many an hour thinking of Luke Ward and wondering what they will be doing at that moment. But never mind I shall visit St. Luke's soon as I have saved up some money for the railway fare as it is such a long way to Croydon from Sheffield. If you ever drop a line to Nurse Scott or Nurse Hume, please remember me to them. Should have liked to have been at Luke Ward when the concert was there, it must have been grand. Some ladies wanting to send me to a convalescent home but I shan't go, there's plenty worse than me that ought to go. Old "Gollywog" is going on fine, not causing me a bit of trouble. So I think I have told you all this time. Please excuse the writing and spelling. Remember me to Sister Luke.

From your sincere friend,

Walter Lee

This word has been included to maintain authenticity. It was commonly used at the time, being the name of a black 'skinned' rag doll – a favourite boys toy. During the 1970s the word was considered a destructive instance of racism against people of African descent and is no longer used.

SNAPS IN THE GARDEN

Peter Kirk and
P. O. Davis.

Daddy 5. This snap was taken during his
first visit to hospital, when every effort was
made to save his leg (sepsio). Amputation was
found necessary on his second visit.

Sonny 6 (a great worker). Sergeant Walker. Daddy 5.

24.

Sergeant Walker & Signaller Simpson.

Oct. 2nd 1915.

War Signal Station
Rose Hearty
Nr Frazerburgh
Aberdeenshire

Dear Nurse G. Pulvertaft,

I was sorry to be away from home when you sent the photo. I came back from leave on Sunday night and went away on Monday so you will quite understand how it is that I have not come to see you. I would have liked very much to see you all before I went away but unfortunately I had not much time. Well I had a good time at home, plenty of fine weather. It was a long journey from the South of England to the North of Scotland. It is very lonely and very cold up here. The village has a population of about 2000 so it is not very large. There are two of us billeted at a small farm which is very nice indeed. Well I must draw now to a close as it is nearly time for me to go on watch. Thanking you very much for the photos and your trouble in doing same. Remember me to all the patients that I may know, and best respects to Sister and all the nurses, accepting of course my best regards for yourself.

Yours truly,

Sig. H. H. Simpson

H.M. War Signal Station
Rose Hearty
Nr Frazerburgh
Aberdeenshire

Oct 22nd 1915

Dear Nurse Palventoft,

It was a strange coincidence, as I had just come off watch 9pm to 1am, and I while on watch somehow or other it flashed through my mind that I would like to know how things were getting on, so I was determined that when daylight came and I had a few minutes to spare I would write and find out, but to my surprise there was a letter awaiting me, so I take the measure to reply to same.

We heard about the raid but it was a day or two later when it reached. We don't see any Zepp. up here, we are quite safe from them, only we have the shipping to contend with. I did not hear Sergt. had gone through an operation, but trust that he is going on well, I was going to write him, but thought that he was probably home, anyway you might give him my sincerest wishes for a speedy recovery and if he has time I would be very pleased to hear from him, just to know that he is going on well. Are there any of the old boys left beside Sergt? How is Nurse Scott, Nurse Jackson and Sister getting on? I expect you will all be pretty busy. Well it's time for me to do another watch so must leave this till I come back.

I have just finished only your lines so will try
and get this letter finished. With regards to station
and its surroundings they are just about the same
only it's very lonely and quiet here up in the
North of Scotland. I don't know what kind of
weather you are having, but here it's very bad,
one continual sheet of rain for hours. Going to and
fro the station we're up to our knees in mud. You
see the station's about 200ft. above sea level and I
you can imagine what it can be like. I am still
in the best of health, hoping you're in the same.
We have plenty of good sea air into our lungs and
makes us sleep, which we get little of. I would
be only too pleased to hear from you on anyone.
Remember me to all giving my best respects to
Nurses and Sister.

Yours Sincerely,
Sig. Hutchinson H. Simpson.

From
Simpson. R.N.

Six, "Taffy" and "Tubby"

29.

SNAPS IN THE GARDEN

43 Martin Lane
Upperthorpe,
Sheffield

Dec 8th

Dear Nurse,

Just a few lines hoping to find you in the best of health as it leaves me at
present. I have had a fine card from Nurse Scott, a view of Brighton. I hear
old Daddy 5 is back again. It's a pity that Sergeant is gone out of the hospital.
He would have come in handy for old Daddy 5. Had a letter from Sister Lulie
saying old No 7 was a bit better. Just now we are having dreadful weather here
with a lot of fog and it prevents me going out and when it's like that I have to
stop in house all day reading and playing games or something like that. I have
not much to do, wish I could work it would be a lot better. As I think
I have told you all this time.

From your sincere friend

Walter Lee

43 Martin Lane
Upperthorpe,
Sheffield

December 23rd

Dear Nurse,

Just a few lines wishing you a very Merry Christmas and a Happy new year.
Am sending you my photo, I don't know whether it is like me or not. I have
sent Sister Luke one. Should like to have been at the hospital for Christmas
but with the trains being so very dear I can't pay the fares but shall be
visiting Croydon somewhere near February when I have saved enough.

So I will now close.

Yours sincerely,

Walter Lee
Sonny (No. 10)

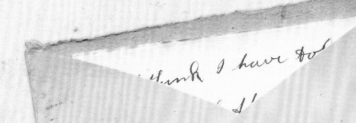

OPERATIONS

During my six months at C.G.H. I was present at six operations in the big theatre. I was always warned to make myself scarce were I to feel faint, but such a thing never happened. Nothing I saw ever affected me in the least, tho' I can hardly say I took much scientific interest. Most of the time I stood and looked on, but occasionally I held salines and handled unsterile objects, not being scrubbed up. Below are the ops. in the order in which I saw them. All were successful. A.C.E.[1] was used as the anaesthetic.

1. Hernia – Dr Wayte
2. Loose cartilage knee (Mortlock) – Dr Adams
3. Appendical abscess (midnight op.) – Mr Newby
4. Shrapnel extraction (Taffy's arm) – Mr Le Blanc
5. Leg amputation (Sonny Lee) – Dr Adams
6. Amputation of finger – Mr Bulcock

With the Sketcher's Compliments.

SAVE THE POOR TOMMY FROM THE FLAPPER

"And you've been through all this for me. Oh, do have a Chocolate!"

E. Crossley
¾
N. Staffs. Regt.
¾
late Yorks. Regt.

MORNINGS WITH THE DENTIST

I'm glad to say I spent but two mornings with the dentist. The first day James (the porter) ushered me into the room: *"Here's nurse!"* was his introduction. *"She's a new nurse and a nice girl – I know her!!"*

The first day I was completely at sea but by the next time I found my duties much less difficult and was able to keep pace with the dentist.

 A.C.E. is an old anaesthetic agent most commonly made up in the ratio: 1 part alcohol, 2 parts chloroform and 3 parts ether.

This was given to me by No 5, a Tommy, wounded at Loos.

Drawn by Q. M. S. Leeming. 13th Siege Battery R.G.A. "Somewhere in France."

Christmas in Luke Ward, Croydon. 1915.

35.

CHRISTMAS IN LUKE WARD
CROYDON GENERAL HOSPITAL 1915

It was said that the one bright spot in Croydon this Christmas was to be found inside the General Hospital. Certainly all the wards were beautifully decorated and for a while patients forgot they were ill.

The week following Christmas, concerts were given every night and between these and trips to the pantomime and pictures, a most enjoyable season came all to quickly to a close for those inside the walls of C.G.H.

James Reid "Scotty," No. 7 and
Fred Mee, No. 8 (seated).

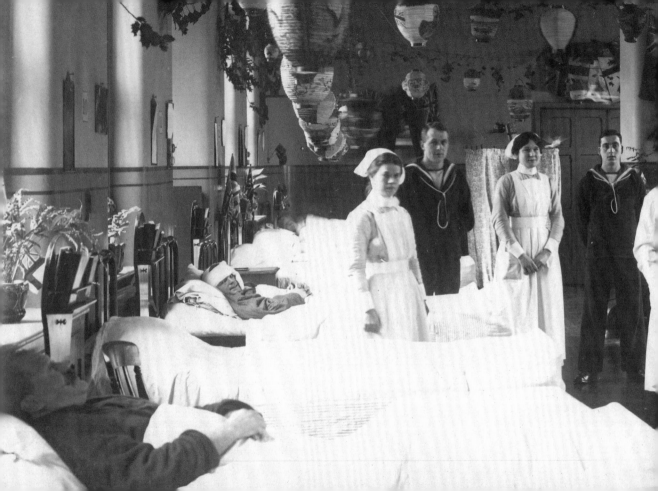

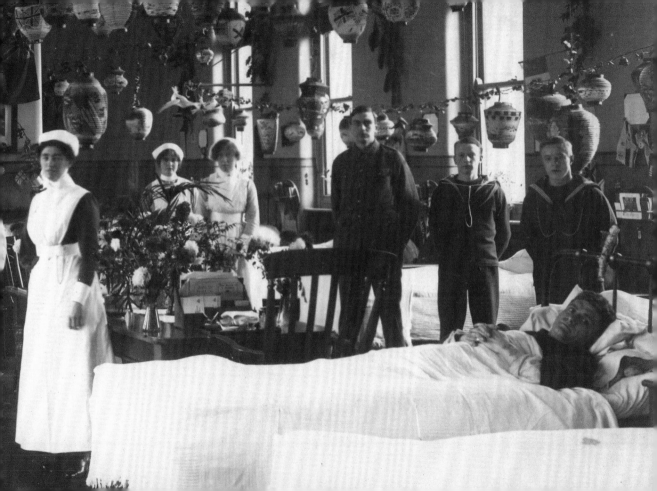

This photo was taken on New Year's Day, 1916, just as some of the convalescent patients were leaving for the pantomime, accompanied by Sister Luke. Nurse Robinson and myself are also seen.

Copy of programme given me by Sonny 3 when he, Sonny 13 Nurse Upton and accompanied them to the Pictures

PALLADIUM NEWS

Vol. 2. No. 2.   Week Ending Jan. 1, 1916.

A WEEKLY PUBLICATION DEVOTED PRINCIPALLY TO THE
ATTRACTIONS OF THE PALLADIUM PICTURE THEATRE, CROYDON.

HAZEL DAWN who plays NIOBE.

NIOBE

Possessing grace to an equal degree as a dancer and poseur Hazel Dawn makes a delightful Niobe She is charming in her woes and amusing in her happy moments. The part gives her ample opportunity to develop all her artistic qualities to their full extent.

Peter Amos Dunn, the president of an Insurance company, take a statue of Niobe home for safe keeping. Electricians leave several coils of wire round the foot of the statue, and soon we see it come to life. Dunn, who is sleeping before the fire, is aroused by sounds emanating from the screen behind which the figure is placed. He investigates and is horrified by what he sees. When the vision flings her arm round his neck and bids him as her master he is petrified with fear, for there is a very self-possessed Mrs. Dunn and a still more self-possessed sister.

When the family, which has gone to the theatre, returns, Dunn hastily sends Niobe upstairs with the clothes which have come for the new governess. Niobe's arrival on the scene clad in various unrelated articles of the governess's wardrobe, is the signal for a small riot. Lored by the dreams of olden days, she escapes in the night to dance upon the greensward. She arouses Dunn in her flight and he gives chase, finally getting back into the house, but not without considerable explanation to his wife.

The situation between Niobe and Mrs. Dunn becomes more and more strained, until finally the latter is on the point of leaving her house. Dunn, in a fury, repulses the clinging Niobe, and she plunges a knife into her heart, expiring in his arms.

The family really return from the theatre and finds Dunn fast asleep before the fire. He is awakened and goes tremblingly over to the screen, to find the statue just as he had left it, whereupon he nearly collapses with joy.

OFF THE REEL.

... of "The Secret Orchard" and ...Conscience" fame, who is due at ... Jan. 3rd, went on the stage at ...company which included Holbrook ...be remembered in our recent ... Boss." At fourteen she was hop...he music of the famous "Spring ...pany of the lady who ran a rival ...Maud Allan, who, by the way, has ...to appear in pictures. Later some...d her to the father of Alice Brady, ...yed the lead in "The Boss" and ...All went well until Blanche smiled. ...Brady threw up his hands and ex...friend, "Great Scot. I can't hire an ...sn't all her teeth yet." Blanche was ...er first teeth at the time. The only ...t is a "fresh air fiend." She ...the house is at dinner time. She ...the open.

...awn, who appears in the famous ...re success, "Niobe." made her stage ...ion, where she figured in "The Pink ...The Joy Ride Girl," and as Xandra in ...Denmark" at the Prince of Wales' ...azel is really her surname. The "Dawn" ... our own Paul Reubens, the composer. ...ely renounced the speaking stage to ...ar with the Famous Players Company.

...M.—I am afraid we cannot adopt ... programme you suggest. However, ... pleased to receive your letter, and ...for your complimentary remarks on our ...nt.

PALLADIUM
(LATE PYKE'S)
NORTH END,
CROYDON.

STOLEN GOODS

Margery Huntley, the heroine (Blanche Sweet) is arrested and imprisoned on a charge of stealing som... which was really taken by a rich kleptomaniac, Helen ...and by her put into Margery's bag when detection ... imminent. After her release Margery becomes a ...nurse, but her prison record hampers her work and she ...to go to Belgium to do good if she can. In this ...country she nurses wounded soldiers of all nationali... in one of the emergency hospitals near the front ...Helen, the kleptomaniac, whom she recognises.

apparently killed from the effect of a Zeppe... Margery argues to herself that she will do no ... even by impersonating the dead girl, whose ... clothes and her ticket to America, which she ... letter of introduction to a wealthy woman in ... had known the kleptomaniac's father.

Helen, however, recovers, and goes to A... find the interloper installed in her place. ...meantime is loved by a young doctor, whose a... has made in Belgium. Helen denounces ... compelled by Margery to confess her own ... past. The young doctor astounded at first ...tions, realises the peculiar temptations that w... Margery, and loyally stands by his sweethear...

Some lines taken from one of Signalman
H.H. Simpson's letter of Jan 5th 1916 referring
to the Natal.

*Were you at hospital for
Christmas? It would be pretty
quiet there, but perhaps more
lovelier than here. It was rather
unfortunate for the Natal to be
blown up at this time of the year.
It was stationed near here.*

*With best good wishes for a
prosperous new year.*

Yours sincerely,
Hutchinson H. Simpson.

The HMS Natal was a Duke of Edinburgh-class
cruiser for the Royal Navy. Launched in 1905 in
Barrow-in-Furness, the ship went on to escort
the royal yacht between 1911-1912 for King
George V. It was regarded as an important
engineering development with larger guns
providing a longer range, greater penetration
and capable of firing 48 rounds per minute,
however it was never used in battle.

On 5th December 1915 whilst anchored in
Cromarty Firth, the Natal suffered from
several internal explosions and sank claiming
approximately 400 lives. The accident, initially
believed to have been an act of sabotage by the
Germans, is now considered as the misfortune
of an unknown spark meeting with a stockpile
of Cordite, a highly unstable propellant that
was used for propelling bullets and shell. Fire
ravished the vessel, causing her to sink within
just 20 minutes after sending a distress signal.

H.M.S. NATAL 1905-1915

TRANSFER TO BRIGHTON

My intention was to remain a month at Croydon, but it is January 1916 and I am still here. I can now say however, that I'm transferring to Eastern General Hospital in Brighton.

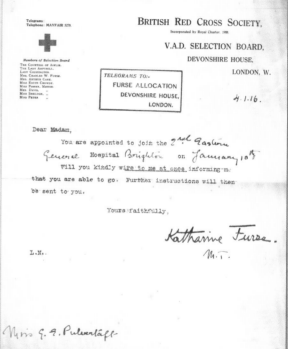

Agreement for V.A.D. Members and others employed in Military Hospitals.

To His Majesty's Principal Secretary of State for the War Department.

1. I *Grace Elizabeth Pulvertaft*

of *London 186*

hereby offer and agree, if accepted by you, to serve at home or abroad in any Military Hospital to which I may be posted in first month of such service to be provisional

2. I am willing to serve under the Rules laid down in the Regulations and Standing Orders for the Territorial Force Nursing Service, as far as applicable.

3. If appointed after the month's provisional service, the period of my service hereunder shall commence as from the day on which I shall commence duty after such provisional service and shall continue until the expiration of six calendar months thereafter, or until my services are no longer required, whichever shall first happen.

4. My pay shall be at the rate of £20 per annum for both my provisional and accepted service, and I shall receive an allowance for maintenance of uniform at the rate of £1 a quarter, payable in arrear. In other respects, except that no gratuity will be payable on the cessation of my employment, I shall receive allowances at the rates and subject to the conditions laid down for the Territorial Force Nursing Service.

5. During the said period I will devote my whole time to my service hereunder, and will obey all orders given to me by superior officers.

6. In case I shall in any manner misconduct myself, or shall be (otherwise than through illness or unavoidable accident) unfit in any respect for service hereunder, of which misconduct or unfitness you or your authorised representative shall be sole judge, you shall be at liberty from and immediately after such misconduct or unfitness to discharge me from further service hereunder, and thereupon all pay and allowances hereunder shall cease.

Dated this 12 th day of *February* 19 16

Grace Elizabeth Pulvertaft (here sign).

Witness to the signature of the said

Grace Elizabeth Pulvertaft
J. O'Reee Carle - Mabine (Witness).

On behalf of the Secretary of State I accept the foregoing offer.

Sidney Browne. M. in C. T. F. N. S.

for Director-General, Army Medical Department.

(s 6200) Wt v. 13529—2029 5000 12/15 H & S G. 15/277

44.

45.

MY FIRST CONVOY

It is 7pm on a chilly February evening and those unfortunate beings know as the night nurses are beginning to stir in their cubicles. The dormitory door opened suddenly and a voice is heard:

"A convoy is due to arrive tonight at 8 o'clock."

Terriers (Territorial Nursing Reserve) and V.A.D.s are duly impressed. *"Can it be possible?"* *"There has been no heavy fighting?"* *"We have not had a convoy for months!"* Such are the remarks on all sides. Downstairs bustle the nurses and after a hasty breakfast they scramble into the ambulance to verify matters for themselves. Everything is correct – beds are prepared and near 11pm the tramp of many feet is heard – the orderlies are marching to the station. "Lights Out!" is heard across the square but little attention is paid to the same call and 15 minutes later the ambulances rumble to the door. "Kings" is our ward and we are to have the stretcher cases. In they come!

Here is a haemorrhage case necessitating immediate operation, here is an injured head, there a shattered limb. Still they come and one by one the other patients blink their eyes, awakened by strange sounds. One man is heard to remark *"When will it end? And all because of one man."*

"When indeed?" is the query on the entire ward. Just after midnight everything is again quiet. The wounded (shell fire) having left France in the hospital ship "Cambia" are now safe in Dyke Road Hospital, Brighton, and washed, warmed and fed. We leave them to enjoy this well earned rest.

NIGHTMARE DAYS OF THE NEW NURSE.

By SYBIL HOLLAND

Well! So I am really a "pro." How funny it sounds! From much acquaintance with tennis courts and golf links I have come to regard the word with some awe, as belonging to one who is master of his art; but the kind of "pro" that I am is of a very different species. This "pro," like the proverbial well-behaved child, must be seen and not heard; she must sink into oblivion and yet always be on the spot when needed; she must neither have an opinion, an aspiration, nor any personal identity, and should never forget that she is a mere nobody.

There are many things that she must do, and still many more that she must not do and the dividing line is not easy to discern. Countless acts are quite criminal from a hospital standpoint, and this particular "pro" has committed every enormity that it is possible to commit. Surely if there were such a thing as a hospital prison she would be lying in its very darkest dungeon.

THAT UNIFORM!

Day 1. – Just fancy me in uniform! Never have I felt so self-conscious since the day I first put my hair up at school. How uncomfortable it felt! The collar scrubbed my neck raw, and the "war cap" entered fully into everything I was engaged on – from the coffee at breakfast to the soup at dinner, from the sterile drum to the lysol baths. Words will not express how lonely, homesick, and ignorant I felt. It seemed that the hospital simply bristled with fully qualified nurses and that I was the only ignoramus among them and the only person who had not lived there since the Flood. I was shown over the hospital and introduced as the "new nurse."

Day 2. – What terrible things I managed to do! First, I picked up a sterile bowl with my unsterile fingers, carefully putting my thumb inside, and then made matters worse by dropping the sterile forceps on the unsterile floor, and opening a sterile dressing with the then unsterile forceps, and touching a dirty dressing with my "scrubbed up" hands, and pouring the saline into an unsterile bowl, and laying the sterile pickers on the unsterile table, and washing the dirty instrument under the wrong tap and rubbing the silver probe with emery paper, and polishing the rust off the forceps until all the plating came off, too.

I followed this by leaving the gas on till the bowls burnt dry, and putting a pin the wrong way into a packet of dressings, and not knowing that a wick, a pack, a drain, a mesh, and a thread mean the same thing; that a sponge has no resemblance to that from which it gets its name, and that in reality it is identical with a wipe, a dressing, a swab, and a gauze; and that neither dirt nor rust is of any consequence on an instrument so long as it is sterile.

I dreamt that night of sterilisation, and awoke with a start, imagining that I had knocked over the sterile dressing-table – but it was only my own unsterile dressing table, constructed by myself out of a packing case, and was somewhat unsteady by reason of my having tried to fix on four legs with three nails.

TRIBULATION

Day 3. – Having forgotten to set my alarm for six, I awoke leisurely at 7.30– the precise time to go on duty. No sleep was ever worth the horrors of that awakening! A bath was quite out of the question, and breakfast should have been by rights, but my hunger got the better of me, and I drank boiling coffee so quickly as to scald my mouth and had a choking fit through trying to do juggling tricks with a very solid roll. Then with breathless haste I reached the ward to find that Sister with her own royal hands had taken a note to matron's office to "report" that I had not appeared on duty. The day began badly, but I determined to make up for lost time, and I was "through" by nine punctually, and was carrying in the nine o'clock cocoas nicely arranged on a tray when the unexpected appearance of the medicine chef in the kitchen, showing some notability over the hospital, so perturbed my equilibrium that I upset the whole bag of tricks over my unfortunate person, soaking my apron and white shoes, and (though this a mere detail) scalding m unoffending feet.

Day 4. – I met the matron on th stairs and said "Good morning," forget ting that it is not "etiquette" for a "pro to take such liberties; she must wait til she is spoken to by superior officers. spoke to another "pro" in the ward i the presence of the surgeon – anothe terrible breach of etiquette; in a fit o absentmindedness sat down to dinne at the table reserved for "sisters," an forgot to clean my knife on my brea ready for the next course. I broke tw thermometers and a medicine glass boiled the scissors, upset the tray o bandages, scarred my arm for life wit pure carbolic, and walked into the dis pensary without knocking.

Day 5. – I went on night duty, from which moment I lived in a perpetua struggle of trying to keep awake at nigh and asleep in the day. My head was i a positive whirl of uncertainty. I neve knew the date, or whether it were to day, yesterday or to-morrow, night o morning. Never has the sun shone mor brightly than it did during those days spent in bed – it was the one brief spe. or real summer we had all last year!

And now the days have ceased t have numbers! Looking back, it seem one long vista – days melt into weeks weeks into months; and so it will b until victory comes and war hospital have a returned to the dust from which they came.

Lce Cpl Davis, Chevion, presented me with this newspaper clipping (left) during my first week in Dyke Road Hospital.

FEBRUARY 16ᵗʰ 1916

I am on night duty and write in bed. At 5pm the unfortunate V.A.D.s are called, for it is Wednesday and we must attend Captain Fletcher's lecture – 'Tis interesting enough but its hard to have to get up two hours earlier than usual. I'm still thinking of the brain hernia (Skinner) in Kings. He seems a wee bit brighter. I do hope all goes well.

Nurse Shannon informed me today that she came from Skibberine. Nurse Wagner knows the Pulvertafts in Cork!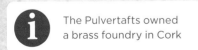 I'm sleepy so good night.

The Pulvertafts owned a brass foundry in Cork

2ND EASTERN GENERAL HOSPITAL "MEDICAL STAFF" BRIGHTON · 1916

269
G.A.WILES
BRIGHTON

51.

Scribbling in the corridor whilst waiting for Nurses Lunt and Dennis, I copied this poem from "The Tatler". Written by an officer at Suez resting after the evacuation of Gallipoli.

AFTERWARDS

To sleep
With quiet heart and mind, a deep
untroubled sleep throughout a night
of peace:

And wake,
Knowing there is no need to take
Up arms against the day to come;
and then

To live
and taste the joy each hour can give,
The joy of life itself - unspoiled;
and so

To sleep
Again, and through the hours to keep
the memory and promise of
the day!

FEBRUARY 20th 1916

I've been home for the first time. I had a night off. 'Twas fine but oh so short. I spent last night in Queen Mary Ward – a vast improvement on Skinner and his vile language!

FEBRUARY 23rd 1916

The night after, saw me in Roberts, Kitchener, etc. – seven wards in all, with Nurse Smith as my companion – never again! I sat in a stone corridor surrounded by screens with a candle for light – I felt absolutely in the blues. Nurse Smith... Well... !

The next night saw me in York and Connaught – not bad – but even Kings with Nurse Lunt seemed preferable. Last night I spent in Red Cross. I saw several of my old Chevion friends – 'Twas my most enjoyable night so far. Block B is infinitely preferable to Block A.

MARCH 9th 1916 – GORDON AND LINCOLN WARDS – 3am

I am getting quite used to night. About time – this is my sixth week! All the same, I do get terribly sleepy, tho' the sensation rarely exceeds 30 minutes now. My present wards are Kelvin and Lister. At present Nurse Clarke is doing nights off as I remain in her sitting room while the one orderly for the block stays upstairs. We are exceedingly slack. There is nothing doing all night and only breakfasts to consider in the mornings – besides of course the washings – but as most men are up this does not mean much. Tonight, for instance, I made a curtain for Sister Macreath, finished a jaconet cover for Nurse Johnston and got Sister's supper as well as my own – these being cleaned away I went round the wards, five in all, I gave drinks where required. After this there was nothing more to be done. Were Nurse Clarke here, we'd be having the most elaborate meals – pancakes etc. But I cannot bother for myself.

Capt. Steinhouser has just been in for his milk – he was suddenly summoned to Kings Ward – A V.D.H. case having been admitted at this early hour. I often supply the staff with this beverage. I keep a supply on, in boiling water so 'tis always ready. Lieut Ross appeared early for his supper. No sooner had the captain departed then Nurse Leburn arrived on the scene saying *"Sister Lovell ought to get six months for her writing."* – and asked me to put the names in the report book as she couldn't make them out – then she spotted my diary and wanted to know what I was saying about her!

The other night – early Monday (6th) to be accurate – my head was getting nearer and nearer my book when............................ the lights went out! I was awake in a moment and I realised that a Zepp raid was in progress. The nearest Zepp passed 25 miles from here so we were hardly in the thick of things.

The sights seen in this hospital are terrible at times. Not long ago, Nurse Clarke called me down to see her patient. I went cheerfully into Gordon to find a man on the floor spinning round and round on his face, waving his arms in all directions and shrieking:

KILL HIM! KILL HIM!!!!!
CALL UP THE COMMUNICATION.
THAT'S DONE FOR ANOTHER.

The men were quite nervous, for he was really violent and had to be moved into a side ward with orderlies in attendance – a bullet through his spine was the cause.

Then again – MacIvor in Kings is dead. Poor old chap. He came over in my first convoy. I remember the night so well. Shrapnel in the head and abscess on the brain was the trouble. MacIvor was a Scotsman and hailed from the Orkneys. When delirious he would lapse into Gaelic and his sister, who came down to see him, could speak no English. Such a nice fellow as he was – and quite young. Whenever questioned as to how he was, it was always – *"Much better, thank you nurse."*

This war...! I must to work. We'll be jolly busy when a convoy turns up – there are so many empty beds.

MARCH 12th 1916

I am back again in Kelvin and Lister Wards – and glad I am too. Block A I do not like. Another convoy has just come in which makes my third experience of the same. Rumours of 85 men reached the night dormitory but only 8 came to Dyke Road and they were admitted to Block B. None turned up here but Nurse Clarke had two admittances so I helped down there. She is certainly very kind. At 2pm when I stole into my cubicle after my second night off – I found biscuits and milk left there by her! I must now put on porridge or rather stir some!

Nurse Johnson.

Night dormitory

ROYALTY AT BRIGHTON.
PRINCESS CHRISTIAN VISITS WAR HOSPITAL.

A TALK WITH HER SON'S SERVANT.

Yesterday afternoon the sick and wounded heroes who pick up the broken threads of their constitution in such a marvellous manner at the great war hospital in Dyke-road, Brighton, were cheered by the visit of an English princess. This is the third time the mother branch of the 2nd Eastern General Hospital has been honoured by Royalty, the visit of their Majesties King George and Queen Mary, and that of H.R.H. Princess and Queen Beatrice being followed yesterday by an informal visit of Princess Christian. It was a charming act on the part of Her Royal Highness, who has been spending a quiet weekend at Brighton, staying with her suite at the Norfolk Hotel, to make the occasion an opportunity of seeing something of the hospital life of the wounded soldiers in Brighton, and her presence was a matter of intense gratification to the patients with whom she chatted in the different wards.

The hospital commanded by Lieutenant-Colonel Rooth, which has quite recently been inspected by the Commander-in-Chief of the district, Sir Leslie Rundle, who made a most favourable report, was looking its best and brightest yesterday, the warmth and cosiness of the wards contrasting pleasantly with the outer world, which was cold with a suggestion of falling snow in the air. Lieutenant-Colonel Rooth, Captain Walker and Lieutenant Ross, of the Administrative Staff, with Miss O'dell Carter, the matron of the hospital, received the Royal visitor at the main entrance as she alighted from her motor-car. A number of the sisters, looking extremely neat and trim in their becoming uniform of the Territorial Force Nursing Service, were lined up on either side of the hall. The Princess was warmly clad in a skirt of dark blue serge, cut rather wide and of practical walking length, and a three quarter coat of plush velour with deep edgings of skunk, the collar and cuffs being of the same pelt. Her small close-fitting toque was trimmed very simply with black wings. Lady Edmondstone was in attendance as Lady-in-Waiting and Mrs. Bridges, of Langdale-gardens, the wife of General Bridges, accompanied the Princess, and looked very charming in a suit of velour du noir and dark fox furs.

IN KING'S WARD

The Royal party, under the escort of Lieutenant-Colonel Rooth, first entered Kings Ward, which is fairly full just now, and Princess Christian stopped at many of the beds to pass a kindly word with the occupant, while the convalescents in this large and handsome ward stood at attention as she passed through. "Nelson," "Prince of Wales," "Connaught" and "York" wards were next visited and an inspection was also made of the operating theatre on the ground floor.

Archdeacon Hoskyns, Chaplain of the Hospital, was chatting at the bedside of one of the soldiers, and was presented to the Princess, who shook hands and spoke for a few moments with him.

The greatest interest was shown by the visitors in the interesting life of the hospital, and the Princess intimated to the Commanding Officer her desire to see a man named Young, a sergeant who is lying ill in "Roberts" ward on the first floor. He immediately offered to have this patient carried down on a stretcher, as her Royal Highness finds it rather trying to climb many stairs. But she would not hear of this trouble being taken, and expressed her determination to make the ascent, which is not an inconsiderable one in this huge building. Sergeant Young was the soldier servant of Prince Christian Victor, the Princess's dearly loved son, and some time was spent by the side of the little cot in kindly words and sympathetic inquires. From the time the Prince joined the King's Royal Rifles until he went out to South Africa to meet his death, Young was in constant attendance upon him, and the sergeant was deeply touched and heartened by the tender thought bestowed upon him yesterday by the mother of that gallant young officer.

"She remembered me," he said delightedly, "and I should have known her anywhere, for she has not altered one bit, unless it is to grow more like her queen mother, Victoria the Good." The soldier's eyes filled with tears as he said this, and there is no doubt the visit revived memories of happier days. For after he lost his Royal master bad times fell upon the sergeant, and he was an invalid for seventeen years, but at the beginning of this war patriotism stirred his blood and he responded to the nation's call, this time joining the East Surreys. He has not been destined to go out on active service yet, as the hardships of camp life brought a return of his old malady. "But when I've got over an operation I am going to have, I expect I shall be all right then, and able to go," he pluckily told one of the visitors yesterday. "French" and "Kitchener" Wards on this floor were also visited, and then the Royal party made their way to the orderly room (so well presided over by Sergt. Major Poole, who was in attendance during the visit), where tea was served to the Princess and her friends.

The notice received of the Princess's intention to visit the hospital was very short, but there had just been time to transform the orderly room formerly known as the old "Nelson" Ward) into a very charming tea room. The green walls harmonized well with the f spring foliage of plants and ferns, and daffodils and narcissi with which the tables were decorated. A silver tea ser and dainty china enhanced the effect, although the preparations had beer quickly made, everything was done perfect taste and refinement in honour this very memorable event. During Miss Ionides, who had accompanied Royal party on their tour of inspec was presented to the Princess, who le something about the gift room, wh is such a great asset in supplying e comforts and auxiliaries for the woun soldiers in this hospital, and in the m agement of which Miss Ionides dev so much time and does such valued w

THE COLONEL'S AUTOGRAPH ALBUM

Before leaving, Princess Christ honoured Lieut.-Colonel Rooth by scribing her name in his autogr album, which already contains the natures of many illustrious and dis guished visitors who the Command Officer has received, including thos the King and Queen and Princess He of Battenberg, the Archbishop of I lines, and others.

Her Royal Highness, in shaking ha with the Administrative Staff, than the colonel for the pleasure her visit afforded, and congratulated him u the fine equipment of the hospital the evident comfort of all the patients

On Sunday the Princess, with L Edmondstone and Mrs. Bridges, the guest of Sir Sidney Greville luncheon, and previous to her arriva the Dyke-road Hospital she had pa visit to the Hove War Hospital Sup Depot and was much interested in work done there.

This verse is often heard, sung by the men in the wards of this hospital.

The Blighty Song

I want to go home
I want to go home
I don't want to go to the trenches no more
Where whizz bangs and trench mortars fall by the score
I want to go 'ome very much
Where the "Alleman" can't get at me.
O my! I don't want to die
I want to go 'ome!

Sister Macreath.

58.

SGT VARDY

Sgt Vardy of the Wiltshire Regiment, belonged to Lister Ward and for a fortnight he was one of my patients while on night duty. Vardy never would get up in the mornings and being a Sgt he evidently expected this to be over-looked. I fear I was most severe and one morning he went without his breakfast! Before he left however he was first out of bed and in the kitchen cooking the breakfast for the entire ward.

Landed at Zeebrugge 7th Oct 1914.
Wounded at Ypres 24th Oct 1914.
Returned to firingline 18th Dec 1914.
Was in Battle. Neuvechappelle in March 19
Festubert May 1915.
Givenchy June 1915. and Loos Sept 19
Wounded at Loos 27th Sept 1915.
Awarded D.C. Card July 1915.
and D.C. Medal, Sept 1915.

This is a section of First line Fire Trench photographed in December 1914, immediately in front of Fleurbaix where Sgt Vardy served with the Wiltshire Regiment.

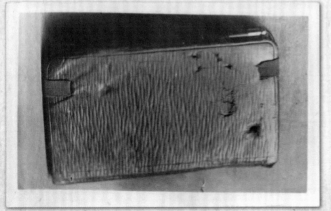

This book no doubt saved Sgt Vardy's life. Carrying the book in his left breast pocket, the bullet passed clean through the book and entered his left breast where it struck a rib.

First Loafer: "Hello, Bill, been fighting?"
Second Loafer: "D'yer s'pose I'm advertisin' stickin' plaster?"

You that have faith to look with fearless eyes
Beyond the tragedy of a world of strife,
And trust that out of night and death shall rise
The dawn of ampler life.

Rejoice, whatever anguish rend your heart,
That God has given you, for priceless dower,
To live in these great times and have your part
In Freedom's crowning hour.

That you may tell your sons who see the light
High in the heavens, this heritage to take:-
"I saw the powers of darkness put to flight!
I saw the morning break!"

Anon

Cpl Whitfield. R.F.A.
Kelvin Ward, March 1916.

I have translated the following taken from a diary found on a dead German by one of the men who is now in Kings Ward, Dyke Rd Hospital, entitled: *"Gottfried Rolls, Stuttgart, Notes on personal experiences (battles, fight, etc.)"*

Aug 16th Marched out of Stuttgart on 16th of August at 8am via Bretler 11am, Bruchsaal 12am, Germeisheim 3pm, one hour for dinner. Journeyed to Frubrücken, detrained at 10.30pm. Marched to Saarbrücken. First bivouac [temporary camp] at 1.30am. Night in the Cecilia School.

Aug 17th Saw the battle field and memorial of 1870. Inspection of guns which were captured from the French.

Aug 18th Crossed from Saarbrücken into Alsace Loraine, past the battlefield of Speichen to Forbach, Rossbrüchen and Spittel. Camp at 5 in the evening.

Aug 19th March from Spittel at 5am. Camp near the enemy at Deefenbach.

Aug 20th Arrayed for first battle. Locality Altdorf, Ersdorf Dieuze. Great battle near Rothalben, Falheim. Obermuköchin ruined by fire. French position at Unternuiköchen. Camp.

Aug 21st Chased the French from Harpll to Marsal. Great battle near Meusen many French dead and wounded – also German.

Aug 22nd Sheltered in Harotell near the Pontier camp.

Aug 23rd Sunday - Marched across the frontier at 7.30am. First town Invercourt. Marched over the Rhine-Marne Canal to Posnor Opalchet near Luneville.

Aug 24th Monday - Marched through Cerres. Great battle the whole day 'til 10pm. The whole night in the open.

Aug 25th Tues: Great battle at 5am continuing 'til evening. Many wounded and killed.

Aug 26th Wed: Drawn up for same battle but could not maintain it. Slept all night in rain in a wood.

Aug 27th In same wood 'til 6pm. Marched to Chambrai. Camped on the frontier.

Aug 28th March from Chambrai to Vic.

Aug 29th In Vic 'til Sept 3rd.

Sept 4th Struck camp 3am. Villages ruined by shell fire. Marched to Bryonoch Anancourt.

Sept 5th Marched through Breiz. Dug trenches.

Sept 6th Sunday. All day in trenches. Heavy cannonade over and near us.

Sept 7th Monday. In fire–trenches near Fevencourt. Then back again. Breiz. Chambrai. Chateau-Salinos and to the hospital.

Sept 8th Started from chatte-Salinos at 7pm. Went through Hambie-Habudingen, Coutil, Bansdorf, Zanbern, Brumatch, Waldenheim, Strassburg and then to the Gangerhaus Hospital 'til Wed: Sept: 23rd. Journeyed to Zuffen-hausen at 5pm. Furlough.

See map overleaf

Sept 25th Went to Unterzuttengen.

Sept 30th Friday. Marched out of Zuffenhausen 8pm. Went through Mannheim, Belbilis, Mayence. Journeyed on Sat: from Oberlahnstein to Koblenz arrived at Trier (Trèves) at 8pm.

Travelled through Luxemburg all night. First stop Cecilie. Dinner at Sedan 10 o'clock. Next through Mexiere, Chorvill and on to Laon. On to Chambrai at 7pm. Journeyed all night. Started for Dalencienne at 8am arrived 10am. Large town. Large camp. Went on to Lille. Everything destroyed by shell fire at railway station. Spent the night in a school. Marched from Lille to Werwig.

Nov 4th Marched from Werwig to Inn-Bruchlen. Marched 'til 2pm. At 6pm marched on thro' Huden, Hordovill, Schloss, Hollebecke to enemy's position.

Nov 5th Here all day. Great bombardment over and round us. Fire trenches in the evening.

Nov 6th Friday. Prepared for battle at 8 o'clock. Thick fog. Heavy cannonade at 10. Lasting 2 hours. At 1.30 stormed the French for 2 hours. Two French officers and 15 men taken prisoners. Back to Kommienes. Marched with the transport from Kommienes to Werwig on Nov 7th and back again to the battle field and fire-trenches.

Nov 8th Lay all day in fire trenches until 10pm – an unforgettable day.

Nov 9th Tues. Sick – dysentery. Resistance of English. Received Iron Cross. Schols - Hollebreche on Sunday.

Nov 15th On to Werwig. Quartered there 'til Nov 20th. Marched to Inn-Brichlen. Standing by.

Nov 24th Fire-trenches 'til Thursday 26th.

Nov 25th First line trenches 'til Wednesday.

Dec 2th Back to Inn-Brichlen. From Inn-Brichlen to trenches 'til Dec 7th.

Dec 10–12th In position. Unforgettable days.

Dec 14th Once more in fire-trenches. Terrific bombardment.

Dec 14–16th In fire-trenches. Frightful cannonade. Unforgettable days. Many dead and wounded. Evening of 16th Dec. back to Inn-Brichlen then two days rest 'til Dec 18th.

Dec 18 – 21st In fire trenches again. Then relieved and back to Werwig. Spent Christmas in Werwig.

Dec 27th At 4pm marched from Werwig to Baed-Fort. New Year celebrated in trenches. Again relieved in huts on the plain 'til Jan 10th. Back to same position.

Jan 15th Relieved – on to Gheluve until Jan 16th.

Jan 16th In position at Grönenbury.

The journal entries finish here. Rest in peace.

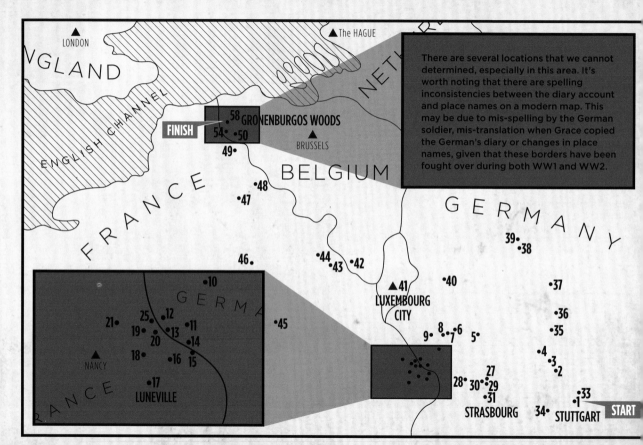

There are several locations that we cannot determined, especially in this area. It's worth noting that there are spelling inconsistencies between the diary account and place names on a modern map. This may be due to mis-spelling by the German soldier, mis-translation when Grace copied the German's diary or changes in place names, given that these borders have been fought over during both WW1 and WW2.

LONDON

The HAGUE

NETHERLANDS

ENGLAND

ENGLISH CHANNEL

FINISH

58 GRONENBURGOS WOODS
54 • 50
49 •

BRUSSELS

BELGIUM

GERMANY

FRANCE

48 •
47 •

46 •

39 • 38

44 • 43 • 42

41 LUXEMBOURG CITY

40

37

36

35

10

GERMA

25 • 12
21 • 19 • 13 • 11
20 • 14
18 • 16 • 15

NANCY

17
LUNEVILLE

RANCE

45 •

9 • 8 • 6
7 • 5 •

4 •
3 •
2 •

28 • 27
30 • 29
31 •

33
1 •
34 • STUTTGART

STRASBOURG

START

This map shows many of the places mentioned in the diary of Grottfried Rolls (the German soldier) shown on the previous page.

LOCATIONS MENTIONED IN DIARY AND SHOWN ON THIS MAP	LOCATIONS MENTIONED BUT NOT SHOWN ON THIS MAP	LOCATIONS MENTIONED BUT CANNOT BE DETERMINED PRECISELY ON THIS MAP	LOCATIONS SOLDIER RETURNED TO, THAT ARE ALREADY MARKED ON MAP

1. Stuttgart
2. Bretten [Bretler]
3. Bruchsal [Brucksaal]
4. Germersheim
5. Zweibrücken [Frubrücken]
6. Saarbrücken [Saarbrüchen] - bivouac/camp
   - Alsace-Loraine = is a region of France
   - Spicheren [Speichen] = historic battlefield located between points 6 and 7
7. Forbach
8. Rosbruck [Rossbrücken]
9. L'Hôpital [Spittle: German name] - camp
10. Diffembach-lès-Hellimer [Deefenbach] - camp
11. Dieuze [Altdorf, Ersdorf Dieuze]
    - Rodalben [Rothlaben, Falheim] = battle that took place between points 4 and 5 when soldier was at point 11
    - Oberneukirchen [Obermuköchin] = is a town near Munich that was attacked
    - Unterneukirchen [Unternuiköchen] = French camp near to Oberneukirchen
12. Hampont [Harpil]

13. Marsal
- Meuse [Meusen] = was a battle not involving soldier
14. Harotell
15. Invercourt
16. Rhine-Marne Canal
17. Posnor Opalchet, Nr. Luneville - marked Luneville as PO is unlocated
18. Serres [Cerres]
19. Chambrey [Chambrai]
20. Vic-Sur-Seille [Vic]
21. Armaucourt [Bryonoch Anancourt]
22. Breiz
23. Fevencourt
- Returns to point 22, then to point 19
24. Château-Salins [Château-Salinos]
25. Hambie-Habudingen
26. Coutil
27. Bansdorf [Batzendorf]
28. Saverne [Zanbern]
29. Brumath [Brumatch]
30. Waltenheim [Waldenheim]

31. Strasbourg [Strassburg]
32. Gangerhaus Hospital
33. Zuffenhausen
34. Unterjettingen [Unterzuttengen]
- Returns to point 33
35. Mannheim
36. Biblis [Beblis]
37. Mainz [Mayence]
38. Oberlahnstein
39. Koblenz
40. Trier [Trèves/Trievs]
41. Luxembourg [Luxemburg] - marked Luxembourg City for journeys reference
42. Sainte-Cécile [Cecilie]
43. Sedan
44. Charleville-Mézières [Mexiere]
45. Cherville [Chorville]
46. Laon
47. Cambrai [Chambrai]
48. Valenciennes [Dalencienne]
49. Lille
50. Wervik [Werwig]

51. Inn-Bruchlen
52. Huden
53. Hordoville
54. Scloss Hollebeke [Hollebecke]
- Goes to unlocated enemy position
55. Kommienes
- Returns to point 50, then to an unlocated battlefield
- Goes back to point 54, then returns to 50
- Moves to point 51, then goes to unlocated fire-trenches
- Returns to point 51, then to unlocated trenches
- Back in fire-trenches
- Returns to point 51, then fire-trenches, then returns to point 50
56. Baed-Fort
57. Gheluve
58. Groenenburgos Woods, Nr. Zillebeke [Grönenburg] - these woods were home to trenches used in WWI, and due to this being the last entry with an abrupt end we believe the German soldier was killed here

2nd Eastern General Hospital R.A.M.C. Staff. Field Day, somewhere in England. 1916.

The Kaiser no doubt
When life ebbs out
Will ride in a flaming chariot
Seated in state
On a red hot plate
Between Satan and Judas Iscariot.

Judas that day
To the devil will say
"My position I now will resign
So put me up higher
Away from the fire
And make room for this favourite of thine."

Gunner J. Paine: Wounded at Armentières
Queen Mary Ward

MARCH 19th 1916 – BY CANDLELIGHT

This morning Croome and I walked to the Dyke.
Yesterday we made all preparations. Spite the fact that
today was Sunday we felt that the change would do us
good – more good than church as we were on night
duty – besides on Sundays alone we get late leave.
Well, we both tackled Sister Ingle during the night and
we both got excused from dinner. At 8am we rallied
forth armed with hard boiled eggs, rolls and fruit.
The day was typical of March with a fresh wind
blowing over The Downs. A little fox terrier greeted us
at the top of the drive and joined beside us the entire
way there and back. We lunched right on the edge of
the Dyke over looking Poynings – a beautiful view
was spread before us and larks were singing overhead.
Seven miles in all is not bad for night duty. Lights have
at last gone up – another Zepp raid I suppose!

> **i** Devil's Dyke is a 100m deep V-shaped valley
> on the South Downs, north of Brighton.

Croome.

Myself.

"Look, Nursie, a Doggie with an Armlet."

APRIL 3rd 1916 – 3AM

I have come to my last night on night duty and I am none too sorry. All the same I feel that I am only now getting used to night work. Varied experiences have been ours these last nights. Never shall I forget last Friday night, lights went out at 9pm and we struggled along by candle light. All the patients had to descend to Chevion where they spent the night – for the most part on the floor! Bed cases were brought down on stretchers. Truly it was a weird sight – morning will bring news of my new dwelling. I wonder where it will be? We all can only wait and see.

71.

APRIL 11th 1916 – INFIRMARY IMPRESSIONS

Here I am in the convent infirmary! I never thought to find myself here but a bad throat developed last Friday, reached a crescendo on Sunday, and as my temperature ascended likewise I had to report sick – to my great disgust!

I'm in a beautiful pink and white room right at the top of the convent, overlooking the garden with the sea in the far distance. Every morning the room is flooded with sunlight and by my bed there is a great vase of pink and red roses – a present from Aunt Bessie. Evans is in the room opposite with a bad chest cold. When the doors are left open we converse together but as Sisters Buchanen and Farren have their rooms in the infirmary great care has to be taken! Nurse Baudin, V.A.D., is my nurse, and one could not ask for better. She is assisted by Sister Clementine, a little French nun. At 6am we are awakened with a cup of tea. 8am sees us with a breakfast consisting of boiled egg, coffee, toast, butter and stewed fruit. At 10 we have a cup of soup, at midday a dinner of chicken or some such thing. 3.30pm brings tea, bread, butter, jam and biscuits. 6.30 supper – an egg, hot milk and fruit. Matron visits us morning and evening, such is a day in the infirmary!

Maiden Aunt Bessie Denroche (Grace's mother's sister) taught nearby.

EASTER 1916.

73.

There's no going back in Devons,
When fighting for their King.
It's on, charge on for Glory,
That to England victory brings.

Pte Wooland 2/7 Devon Cyclists
Queen Mary Ward

8 A.M. MAY 21.
"Oh you shut up! It's only 7
really, I shall have another
hour."

DAYLIGHT SAVING AT
SLOCUM-IN-HOLE.

75.

66757

THE ROYAL SUSSEX.

Who were the Boys when the Battle waged hot,
Dashed to the Front, with a cheery "What-What",
Barged into the Foe and gave them the Knock,
THE SUSSEX!

Who were the Boys when the day looked black,
Hung on to their trench and broke the foe's back,
With a Shot for a Shot and a Crack for a Crack,
GOOD OLD SUSSEX!

Who were the Boys at the River Aisne Dust-up,
Beat back the Hun Guards and smashed up their Krupps,
And at the end of the day were still "Thumbs Up,"
DARE-DEVIL SUSSEX!

Who were the "Men of Iron" that Lord French meant,
When he said that their Line neither "Broke nor Bent,"
Why the Boys of that Grand Old County Regiment,
THE ROYAL SUSSEX!

Who are the Boys that are fond of the "Gals,"
True to their County and true to their "Pals,"
And who made the Germans scoot like hell,
HOT STUFF – THE SUSSEX!

Who were the Boys when they heard England's Call,
Left their loved homes and gave up their all,
For the Motherland ready to fight till they fall,
NOBLE SUSSEX!

Who are the "Fighting Blood" Boys on the Hill,
Training to get fit to lick Kaiser Bill,
Who are the Boys when they Hit–Hit to kill,
SOME FIGHTERS – THE SUSSEX!

Then cherish the Memory of the Boys who fell,
And Honour the Wounded who have grim tales to tell,
Of Mons, Aisne, Festubert, Loos, Neuve Chapelle,
HONOUR THE SUSSEX!

Then a Rousing Cheer for the First, Second, Third,
Fourth, Fifth, Sixth and Seventh Boys too,
If they all Pull Together with the Eighth, Ninth and Tenth,
Nought shall conquer the RED, WHITE and BLUE.

B. WINTON, 1916

Pte Miles and his wool work (occupational therapy).

CONCERT: WITH APOLOGIES TO THE ARTISTS

Given by the staff and patients of Gordon Ward – May 1916

1. Opening chorus: "The Gordon Boys" – <u>Patients</u>
2. Song: "My Fairy Queen" – <u>Nurse Pulvertaft</u>
3. Comic song: "I Don't Like Work and Never Did" – <u>Pte Dunston</u> (day orderly)
4. Song: "The Deluge" – <u>Cpl Flood</u>
5. Duet: "Love Me Little. Love Me Long." – <u>Nurse Lunt & Nurse Smith</u>
6. Humorous song: "Hip-I-ady-I-ay" – <u>Pte Chatfield</u>
7. Song: "When Day Dawns" – <u>Pte Whenday</u>
8. Reading: "My Favourite Newspaper" – <u>Cpl Reynolds</u>
9. Song: "I Love Them All" – <u>S. Lovell</u>
10. Song: "Sing Me To Sleep" – <u>Pte Overden</u> (night orderly)
11. Humorous song: "You Can't Diddle Me!" – <u>Sgt Major</u>
12. Duet: "The Dinky Cap Brigade" – <u>Pte Miles and Pte Bailey</u>
13. Song: "I've Got My Eye On You" – <u>The Matron</u>
14. Song: "The Garden of Roses" – <u>Nurse Gardiner</u>
15. Monologue: "Ronuk❶ and How To Use It" – <u>Mrs Green</u> (char lady)
16. Song: "Bid Me Goodbye For Ever" – <u>Sgt Hollenden</u>
17. Song: "I'll Carve My Way To Glory" – <u>Cpt Bate</u>
18. Closing chorus: "I'm Longing For My Dear Old Home Again" – <u>Patients</u>
19. God Save The King

❶ Ronuk was a popular brand of cleaning products.

JUNE 4th 1916 – "KELVIN" AND "LISTER"

I am now working at Kelvin and Lister. Shankie is with me. She has just come off night – before that I had Kitty Jones.

For almost a fortnight I was theatre pro. The work did not appeal to me in the least. I told Sister so and she said she knew it. Medical cases I infinitely prefer to any others. It is now just ten and everyone is very quiet. I write in bed – it's a terrible night – so cold and windy so I'll now to sleep.

Halls.   Brooker.   Frain.   Blackman.   Dooney.

Bowles.   Whitfield.   Jones.   Frain.

JUNE 8th 1916

Yesterday was my half day. Tanner, Whittle, Page and I bused to Rottingdene and walked over The Downs to Brighton. We finished up with a great tea at Fullers.

The walk was lovely – The Downs rolling away on our right with the sea stretching as far as the eye could see to the left.

I meant to give a full description of my time today in Star Side Ward but Evans hauled me into the corridor to hear a nightingale and its now 10pm – good night.

JUNE 13th 1916

We had our memorial service for Kitchener tonight. 'Twas held in Queen Mary Ward. Never have I known such an impressive sight. The ward was packed with nurses, R.A.M.C. and wounded. As "last post" sounded it seemed as though the end of all had come. Afterwards a Chevion man came to me and said: *"What if Kitchener is not dead?"* I wonder.

Memorial Service

TO

THE LATE FIELD-MARSHAL

EARL KITCHENER, K.G.,

(SECRETARY FOR WAR),

AND

The Gallant Officers and Men who have
laid down their lives for their Country
in the recent Great Naval Battle.

HELD IN

The Hospital Church,

DYKE ROAD, BRIGHTON,

TUESDAY, JUNE 13TH, 1916,

At 6.30 p.m.

ORDER OF SERVICE.

. . THE . .
DAILY ROUTINE

OF A

SOLDIER'S LIFE

TO THE

Titles of Well-known Hymns.

6.30 a.m.	REVEILLE	"Christians awake."
6.48 a.m.	ROUSE PARADE	"Art thou weary, art thou languid?"
7.9 a.m.	BREAKFAST	"Meekly wait and murmur not."
8.15 a.m.	C.O.'s PARADE	"When he cometh."
11.15 a.m.	SWEDISH DRILL	"Here we suffer grief and pain."
1.0 p.m.	DINNER	"Come, ye thankful people, come."
2.55 p.m.	RIFLE DRILL	"Go, labour on."
3.15 p.m.	LECTURE BY OFFICER	"Abide with me."
4.20 p.m.	DISMISS	"Praise God from whom all blessings flow."
5.0 p.m.	TEA	"What means this anxious, eager throng?"
6.0 p.m.	FREE FOR THE NIGHT	"O Lord, how happy we shall be!"
6.20 p.m.	OUT OF BOUNDS	"We may not know, we cannot tell."
10.0 p.m.	LAST POST	"All are safely gathered in."
10.15 p.m.	LIGHTS OUT	"Peace, perfect peace."
10.30 p.m.	INSPECTION OF GUARD	"Sleep on, beloved."

H.W.

JUNE 20th – 27th 1916

Eight days holiday! I went to Ilfracombe, Devon

82.

JULY 4th 1916

I have just returned from a visit to Mrs Soltall, Worthing. I cycled out behind Shoreham and Lancing and had quite a good time – never met so many soldiers in all my life!

Since last writing in this book I have had a varied time. I came back from Ilfracombe and was straight away posted to Stanford Road – "George and Edward" being my special property – I'd not been there three days before I was ordered to Block A – top floor – such a rabbit warren it is – I spend my time running races round stone corridors – I hear that a convoy has turned up tonight – also that Kelvin, Lister, Lincoln, Gordon and Scott are to be turned into Officers Wards so we are in for runs. Everyone is flying off to assist with this convoy. We were full up before so can't be much busier now. Good night.

JULY 5th 1916

We have had a day – Marlbow emptied for spring cleaning – was packed with convoy men – likewise Kitchener. All the men were wounded last Saturday and awful wounds they are – the worst I have ever seen. Tonight I was the one V.A.D. on for seven wards!

Nurse Shannon invited me to tea this afternoon. We had strawberries and cream as this morning a supply was sent into the hospital and we existed on the same without making any impression!

JULY 6th 1916

"You are in the same regiment as my brother?"
said Capt. Hutchinson to a Scottie who had
just arrived from France... *"Do you know Major
Hutchinson?"*

"Yes Sir." replied the man.

"How is he getting on?" was the MO's query.

*"I saw him shot down on Saturday last – he's
dead sir."* was the reply.

Such is war.

JULY 8th 1916

Chaos and confusion yesterday morning as we
went on duty in the pouring rain. Strings of
ambulances approached the hospital – a convoy
was arriving – Block B, emptied for officers, was
promptly filled with men – the most ghastly cases.

Hardly were these men admitted than a wire
came through. The officers were to arrive
the same evening. The first convoy must be
transferred – where were they to go?

The only way out of the difficulty was to pack
everyman anyway on the mend to a convalescent
home. The result was that men – stretcher cases –
were arriving at the bedside of men just getting
up to go off convalescent. This continued for the
afternoon – I was on duty from 7 until 7.

This morning the work was ————— !
However I'm to bed for the afternoon – I will
not see duty again till 5.

JULY 12th 1916

"Something attempted, something done has earned a nights repose."

I've been on since one and feel like that.

I like some of the new convoy men exceedingly – they are most amusing – one told me tonight that "the night attacks" prevented him from sleeping – the first started at 4.55am prompt when he was awakened with a mouthful of soap.

Terrible things must be happening in France. One told me that no mention is made of the huge losses in this advance. Three divisions to his left were almost wiped out and they themselves only advanced 100 yards instead of 4500.

It's a terribly wet night – goodnight.

JULY 13th 1916

In a military hospital:

Nurse to new patient: *"Did the orderly take your temperature my boy?"*

Uneasy patient: *"Dunno miss, but I pinched my chums baccy just now!"*

A TESTIMONIAL!......................

WITH THE
BEST OF
WISHES
· TO ·
NURSE PULVERTAFT.

Pte. S. Snowley,
N. Staffs.
Regt.

ALAS! POOR
HERR VON
YORICK!

"during the "Septender" July, 1916

Rifleman H. Baker,
13th Batt. Rifle. Brigade
To
N. Pulvertaft.

I wish here to express my sincere thanks to the Sisters and Nurses of Roberts Ward in the 2nd Eastern General Hospital for their kindness to me whilst an inmate of the above Institution

JULY 14ᵗʰ 1916

A notice was put up on our board to the effect that the nursing staff was invited to tea in order to meet the voluntary workers of the hospital.

Accordingly Evans and I made our way to the N.C.O.s' mess room which had been converted into a beautiful tea room. To start with we were the only V.A.D.s. We were seated at a table packed with sandwiches, cakes and strawberries and cream. Later Miss Ionides appeared and introduced us to the Duchess of Norfolk – with whom I had the honour of shaking hands. I was introduced as:

"...the girl who came all the way from Ireland to help!"

Tonight the men were going through their experiences at The Front. Sergt Cook who probably goes convalescent on Monday said: *"If I go convalescent, I'll probably return to France in a month or so and I dread going back. Out their we do not live, we merely exist."*

Another told me that in trench warfare the Germans were vastly superior to us – their aerial torpedoes were terrible. In fact, all their shells were made to have the most diabolical sounds.

Baker wrote to nurse Shannon today and desired to be remembered to: *"...the fair nurse whom he helped to make the beds."* Behold myself!

JULY 15th 1916

Tonight I saw a rather interesting souvenir – Knox R.I.R. showed it to me – a slip of paper torn from a message book and signed by a Capt: *"Regret impossible to send more men – consolidate position on left flank towards Pozières."*

Only the other day a motor dispatch rider handed this to Knox – he himself being wounded – five minutes later Knox was wounded and unable to carry out orders.

JULY 17th 1916

I had my first battle today with Page – 'Twas fine!

This message I heard from Kitty Jones – she seems to be enjoying herself:

"Yesterday afternoon I spent with the Lowers. I met Colonel Lowers and Lt. Colonel Stephenson. Later we went to see poor Hopewell at the Howard Home."

JULY 30th 1916

My candle has gone out and it is after 10, so I write in darkness. This is only a line on my 21st birthday. I slept 3 hours at home this afternoon. When will the war be over!?

"ONE OF THE GIRLS."

THE PREVAILING EPIDEMIC.
"CONSCIENTIOUS OBJECTORS."

JULY 31ST/16.

WITH THE BEST OF WISHES
— TO —
NURSE G. E. PULVERTAFT.

THE ALL-HIGHEST WAR-LORD.
KNOCK GENTLY.

Turks (Ottamen Empire) allied to Germany suffered a series of defeats from Allied Forces. Lawrence of Arabia led the Arab revolt.

This poem, entitled 'Screens' was written by a Tommy in No.1 General Hospital, France. The original is to be found in Whittle's book.

They put the screens around the bed,
A crumpled heap I saw him lie;
White counterpane and rough dark head,
These screens – they showed that he would die.

They put the screens about his bed,
We might not play the gramophone;
And so we played at cards instead,
And left him lying there – alone.

The covers on the screens are red,
The counterpanes are white an' I clean;
He might have lived an I loved an I red,
But now he's done for at nineteen.

An ounce or more of Turkish lead,
He got his wounds at Suvla Bay;
They've brought the Union Jack to spread,
Upon him when he goes away.

He'll want these three red screens no more
Another man will get his bed.
We'll make the row we did before
But – love – I'm sorry that he's dead.

Edward Crossley – a patient with considerable artistic talent and good humour – regularly contributes to my diary.

Edward Crossley No. 23409
Sunshine Home
Hassocks

Dear Nurse,

Just a line to let you know how the world is using me since I left your kind care.

I am pleased to say that they have sent me to a very beautiful home indeed, it seems to be a private Convalescent Home as there appears to be one or two invalid ladies, and there seems to be about 24 Tommies.

I had a splendid drive in a most luxurious motor car, there were 5 of us for Sunshine Home, and as a few of them were not ready I had a drive around Brighton with the nurse on a shopping expedition, we arrived at the home about 1 o'clock.

I wish to say here how sorry I am to have to leave all the good friends which I have made at Dyke Road, and especially the nurses, and wish to express to you my sincere thanks for the interest taken in the little talent which I possess with regard to sketching, and I can assure you that whilst I am here I will do my best to add a few more to your collection.

I am sorry I was rushed away so early that I could not thank you personally.

I would like here to ask a favour of you, you will probably have seen one of the postcard groups of the 60 men who went to Hassocks on Friday, I understand that they are on sale at 2d each in the Recreation Room, would you mind obtaining for me 3, I am enclosing 6 stamps in payment, I intended getting them before leaving but had not the opportunity.

Kindly give my best respects to my old friends still left in "Roberts" Ward.

Also I wish to be remembered to Sister Smith, Nurse Shannon and Nurse Williams, hoping I may be privileged to see you again before going home on furlough.

I will now conclude, hoping you may be blessed with the best of health to carry sunshine into the lives of other men, as you have into my life.

With the best of wishes,
I remain,
Yours sincerely,

Edward Crossley

Shone & Phillips.

Evans & Croome.

Myself & Thatcher.

AUGUST 2nd 1916

I've just been painting Shankies throat. Evans did not approve. She lives next door to Shank and said I couldn't be doing it in the correct style or Shank would be sick. So she came in looking most ferocious armed with a toothbrush as spatula and between us we performed the operation! I believe I shall be going on nights soon worse luck!

> **i** 'Painting the throat' refers to the application of a dilute antiseptic (sometimes iodine) to treat conditions such as sore throats, ulcers, thrush, tonsillitis, etc. A brush was used to apply the antiseptic to the inside of the throat.

AUGUST 18th 1916 – MIDNIGHT – KINGS

I'd only just prepared supper for Lock and me
upstairs and wondered why she did not come up.
Going into the kitchen I glanced down into
Connaught kitchen of which the door was open.
Something had happened.

Through the door I could look into the theatre
where the trolley was being prepared while Evans
was busily engaged filling hot water bottles.
A man had haemorrhaged suddenly, though it was
expected after his operation.

I've just seen him – a ghastly colour – and now
since starting this account he has died on the table
– such is one of the experiences of a V.A.D.

SOME SALT FOR HIS TAIL
Poor little Charlie Chaplin, he's breaking his heart at
Lost Angeles. His salary's grown so big, poor chap, they
won't let him wear a khaki cap although he's terribly
anxious to do it. He's written to say so – pass the cruet.

94.

95.

(481)
G.A. INNES
BRIGHTON

DO WE LOOK DOWNHEARTED!

UR WOUNDED HEROES FROM BRIGHTON HOSPITALS ENTERTAINED AT HASSOCKS TEA GARDENS 21/7/16

96.

"The Girl who took the wrong Turning."

H. Crossley

OPERATIONS

Hernia – Stanford Road
Old scar in leg – Stanford Road
Haemorrhoids – Stanford Road
Haemorrhoids – Stanford Road
Mastoid – Block A
Varicocele – Stanford Road
Tenotomy – Stanford Road
Haemorrhoids – Stanford Road
Scrapping of toenail – Stanford Road
Amputation of finger – Block A
Amputation of finger – Block A
Shrapnel in arm – Block A
Shrapnel in leg – Block A
Hydrocele – Block A
Hernia – Block A
Excision of Kidney – Block A
Varicose veins – Stanford Road
Shrapnel in Leg – Stanford Road
Shrapnel in Hand – Stanford Road
Cyst in hand – Stanford Road
Shrapnel in Shoulder – Block A
Machine gun bullet in leg – Block A

"The Mayor and Corporation"

HUNS ACROSS THE SEA.

Pte. E. Crossley
N. Staffs
Regt.

98.

A TRUE INCIDENT OF THE GREAT WAR, 24/8/1916

It happened during the early part of the war, and is an excellent example of the ingenuity, or rather, deep cunning of the enemy. That masterly piece of strategic generalship, the withdrawal of the British from the centre had been accomplished a few days previous to the night of which I shall write, and we now found ourselves firmly established near to Armentières, and a little in front of the village of Houplines. Running from West to East is a very deep ditch which we called, for the want of a better name, the Nullah.

This Nullah, strange as it may sound, was held by both British and Germans.

You see, the Nullah portion of our trenches faced approximately North, and ran parallel to the Nullah for a mile or more, and then faced East, with the enemy's lines encircling the outer-angle, or point, of the right-angle thus formed, and at the same time cutting and commanding the Nullah further East. So you see, at least I hope you do, that both sides held the Nullah. Each party sent out at irregular intervals, reconnoitring patrols to ascertain what was "going on" at the other end, and thereby "harps my tale".

At about 10pm on the night in question one of the sentries informed me that at least two of the enemy were approaching his post, evidently one of the afore-mentioned patrols, and asked for instructions. I gave them and he acted accordingly. As soon as the first comer was within striking distance the sentry, with the rapidity of a lightning flash brought the butt of his rifle in contact with his enemy's head with sufficient force to kill an ox. Needless to say the victim fell, killed as we thought, before a word of alarm or even a groan, could escape him. Notwithstanding the rapidity and silence that characterised the whole incident, the other had however been warned in time, for no trace could be found of him, although patrols marched everywhere. The patrols having returned, I decided to search the "dead man" myself; and what do you think I found? A Prussian Officer? No! A clever, ingenious, Oh! What adjective will do it justice? Cunningly contrived "Mechanical Toy!" Space forbids a detailed description of this – Yes! – uncanny piece of mechanism. Let this suffice – it was made of aluminium; dressed in a German uniform and accoutrements; with limbs and movement which, with the aid of darkness, were sufficiently life-like or human, to deceive us.

The object of the ruse is obvious. By its aid the manipulator gained the information he required, – position of our sentry-post; and assurance of our vigilance, – without, in the least endangering his own life.

A remarkable, though none the less true, instance of German cunning.

Sgt J.A. Cheshire
R. Warwick Regt. 4th Division

TRANSPARENT
REGGIE.

PTE. E. CROSSLEY,
N. STAFFS.
REGT.
[LATE OF YORKS.
REGT.]
(Green Howards)

THERE WILL BE DREAMS AGAIN

THERE will be dreams again! The grass will spread
Her velvet verdure over earth's torn breast;
By ragged shard, half-hid, where rust runs red,
The soaring lark in spring will build her nest.

There will be dreams again! The primrose pale
Will shelter where the belching guns plowed deep;
The trees will whisper, and the nightingale
Chant golden monodies where heroes sleep.

There will be dreams again! The stars look down
On youthful lovers – Oh, first love, how sweet!
And men will wed, and childish laughter crown
Life's awe – compelling miracle complete.

There will be dreams again! Oh, thou forlorn
That crumbling trench or the slow-heaving sea;
Hath snatched thy dead – Oh, pray thee, do not mourn!
There will be dreams – thy loved shall come to thee!

Mabel Hillyer Eastman

A NIGHT IN THE LIFE OF A "KINGS" V.A.D. NIGHT DUTY

8.00pm: Arrive on duty and distribute suppers – cocoa and bread and butter

Erect dug out and searched up empty dressing tins

Fill sterile water can and put on stove

Lay breakfast table

Clear lockers

Lights out

Soak Bed Pans

Wash up supper things

Make and boil swabs

Cut up stack

Fetch milk from Block B

11.15pm: Help prepare V.A.D.s supper in boardroom upstairs

Clear supper and prepare Terriers

12.30am: Rest!

2.00am: Cut bread and butter, prepare eggs, tea etc for breakfast

3.00am: Tea (V.A.D.s)

3.30am: Tea (Terriers)

4.00am: Washings

6.00am: Breakfasts

Such is an uneventful night for the King's V.A.D.

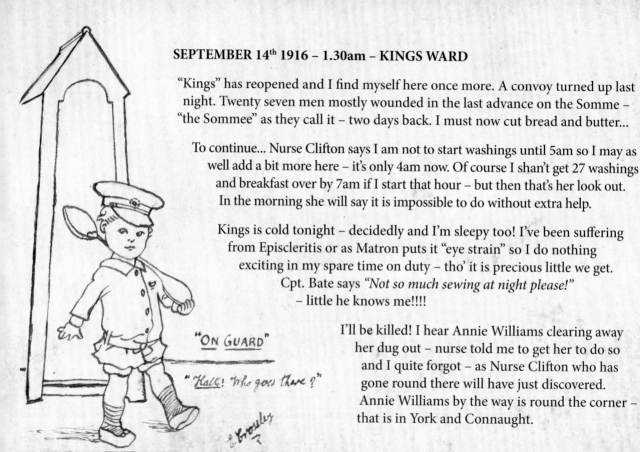

SEPTEMBER 14th 1916 – 1.30am – KINGS WARD

"Kings" has reopened and I find myself here once more. A convoy turned up last night. Twenty seven men mostly wounded in the last advance on the Somme – "the Sommee" as they call it – two days back. I must now cut bread and butter...

To continue... Nurse Clifton says I am not to start washings until 5am so I may as well add a bit more here – it's only 4am now. Of course I shan't get 27 washings and breakfast over by 7am if I start that hour – but then that's her look out. In the morning she will say it is impossible to do without extra help.

Kings is cold tonight – decidedly and I'm sleepy too! I've been suffering from Episcleritis or as Matron puts it "eye strain" so I do nothing exciting in my spare time on duty – tho' it is precious little we get. Cpt. Bate says *"Not so much sewing at night please!"* – little he knows me!!!!

I'll be killed! I hear Annie Williams clearing away her dug out – nurse told me to get her to do so and I quite forgot – as Nurse Clifton who has gone round there will have just discovered. Annie Williams by the way is round the corner – that is in York and Connaught.

"ON GUARD"

"*Halt*! Who goes there?"

103.

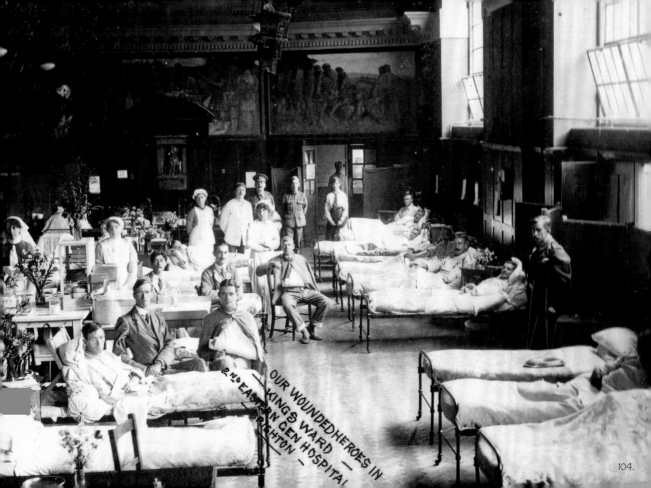

OUR WOUNDED HEROES IN
KING'S WARD
2ND EASTERN GEN HOSPITAL
BRIGHTON

104.

Another poetic contribution to my diary from Sgt Parker......

FEET OF THE YOUNG GIRLS

Now the chords of strife are sounding, now the world resounds with blows,
While above the turmoil comes a cry of pain.
Now the young girl's ears are opened to a call that each one knows,
Means sinking self till peace returns again.
Away with clubs and racquets! Put the court and links behind you!
Burn engagements books and lock your "den" outside!
Burst free from any trammel that would hinder you or bind you.
The call has come and will not be denied.

Ay - you waited not, nor tarried, well we know it who have met you,
In Egypt, Malta, France or further east, our debt is now so heavy that we never
    can forget you.
For we never can repay you in the least,
Were we stricken down with fever? You were there to calm our raving.
Racked with torment? And what could be done, you did.
Infection, hardship, all and any unknown terrors having light-heartedly your
    private troubles hid.

Do you know that cleaning station not so far behind the "line"
Where shattered forms are hurried night and day,
While the deep reverberations of our "heavies" give the sign.
That for all of these the price is yet to pay?
See the patient's glances following the Sisters on her rounds.
She's the first real bit of England they have seen –
And tho' their whitened lips cannot be heard to utter sounds,
They render her the homage of a queen.

Do you know that white - enamelled, shinning, spotless Red Cross train?
And the jar that tells the "points" are being passed?
How every jolt is echoed by a sharp, hoarse gasp of pain,
While the fixed forced smiles are broken down at last.
But only for a moment – for the nurse comes past the cots.
(on the music in the rustle of her dress!)
While she is there the track seems cleared of rough uneven spots,
    and the pain is undeniably less.

Do you know that group of clustered tents where fever cases come
(Look! The mirage dances far across the plain!)
Where the Sisters converse merges in the flies incessant hum.
Punctuated now and then by cries of pain?
Of eleven heads and loving hearts sufficed to stay Deaths hand,
(Today-tomorrow-man is here but grass, and now the oven's flames are fierce,
    by breath of warfare fan'd),
From out their care, no life would ever pass.

Do you know that one time hotel on the beach at Wimereux
And the long, low huts that nestle close beside?
How many hundred cases have the sisters sent through
To Blighty, to the Channel's other side.
They share the 'winners' pleasure when the steamer list comes round
And sympathise with those who stay behind.
Their cheerfulness and never-failing kindness must abound
When things are roughest – grit and love combined.

Do you know the Umpteenth General anywhere on England's shore
A school, or public building in the past
Where gently nurtured women tend the jetsam of the War?
Thrice lucky Wrack on Blighty's sea shore cast!
They ask no thanks nor honour, seeking no reward or praise
Save the knowledge in themselves of duty done
Unsparingly unselfish spending either nights or days
In serving honour to them everyone.

You may be here in England you maybe out abroad.
Where ever you may be it's just the same.
As in peace time on the sword, so in wartime in the ward
You are straining every nerve to win the game.
Matron, Sister or probationer, St John's or V.A.D.
One and all the splendid nursing service through
Tho' we don't give in to Germans to you all we bow the knee,
You've "done" a bigger "bit" than we could do
Australian, Canadian, or the home grown breed of Britain.
The result of all your work shall age proclaim.
Yours the hands that healed the tissue where the German steel had bitten
Yours the touch that helped the bone where hurting shell had smitten
On the first page of the records of this would war be it written
That the Red Cross called for you and so you came.

J. Parker 17.7.1917

SEPTEMBER 18th 1916 – IN BED

A convoy arrived in at 10pm last night, of course 'twas pouring rain and a Sunday and of course I'd been to church in the morning and sat or rather slept through the sermon, arriving back here at 1pm absolutely starving! I boldly marched to the kitchen and demanded something to appease my hunger, where upon I was presented with a stale jam sandwich and I returned to the night dormitory well satisfied.

That church was rather a farce. I went to the congregational led by Williams and Wedekind. We were marched to the front and Williams sat just behind us. She shoved a large hymn book between my back and the pew and whenever my head dropped she would pull it away and thus rouse me from my slumber. They say I slept through the sermon and disgraced myself by talking in my sleep – but then I never attempted to remain in for a sermon before.

Last night's convoy brought 16 to Kings. A 5th Battalion Canadian amongst them C.M.R. who told me that his Battalion was moved from Ypres and entered the Somme trenches on Wednesday last.

I went up to the stewards stores last night and ran into a number of orderlies. One of them unburdened himself to me stating that news of a convoy arrived after all the orderlies had been granted late passes – accordingly they had to be hunted up by bicycle – only 15 came to light – *"Rotten luck when one's out with one's girl"* was his verdict.

I'm sleepy so finie for today!

SEPTEMBER 21st 1916

It's after 10am and I get up at 3.30pm in order to meet my brother Robin in Newhaven, so this is only a line. Another convoy turned up last night or rather early this morning. It was timed to arrive at 1.45am and it never appeared until 4 – just when we were about to start washings! We had ten in Kings and now there is but one empty bed. I'll have some work.

The store orderlies were again on duty. Corporals Tedy and Smith consider that...... *"These are some quite nice nurses on nights just at present."*

I nearly got my head taken off twice. Once for trying to smuggle Lieutenant Ross a cup of tea at 2am when the poor man had been up all night, and again in the later morning when I made tea early for an operation case and Dunstan helped himself to a mugful.

So I suppose I'm accused of flirting both with the Quartermaster and the Day Orderly!

SERGEANT P. COSTELLO, D.C.M.

Sergeant P. Costello, D.C.M., Scots Guards, died at the 2nd Eastern General Hospital, Brighton, on September 23rd from wounds received in France on September 16th. Prior to his death he underwent an operation, as a result of which his arm was amputated. He had served six years in the Army on the outbreak of war, and left England with the original Expeditionary Force. He was wounded on October 6th, 1914, at the battle of the Aisne, and 11 months later left for the front a second time. He received his D.C.M. on June 5th. He was 29, and leaves a widow and one child, who reside at 29, Lutwidge-street, Preston. Before joining the Army he was employed as a weaver at a local mill.

✳

A patient in Kings.

SEPTEMBER 25th 1916

I'm in bed. I'm eating soft biscuits and drinking milk. I've got a cold and have dosed myself with quinine and I am about to paint my throat! Sounds cheerful! However Nurse Gardner has lent me the following which is well worth enjoying.....

Anzac Ward: 6am Any Old Morning
By J.R. Parker

Awake! Nurse Gardner into bowls of white,
Has poured the water, ere the sky is light.
And stirred her patient patients from their sleep,
Before the coming day succeeds the night.

And as she stands there, those who slept before,
Ejaculate with fervour, troubles and more,
Thou knowst how little while we have to sleep,
and once awakened can no longer snore."

But with hard heart and work inflamed eye,
Nurse Gardener draws each several bedstead nigh.
And answering their dismal plaints and moans,
With pity-lacking speech doth make reply.

"Come, wash yourselves, what boosts it to repeat
How time is slipping underneath our feet.
Bad eggs and sloppy porridge wait for you,
Why fret about them if the tea be sweet."

"After your breakfast underneath the shed,
Although you may drop bread crumbs in the bed.
Right easy shall you lie throughout the day,
Fell sleep revisit each unworthy head."

Oh make the most of what ye yet may spend,
Before to convalescence ye ascend.
Then back to marches, packs and shells galore,
Sans bed, sans sleep, sans nurses and — Sans End."

> ## " Oh don't Mr Carter Don't be so silly – you're untidying my hair!

SEPTEMBER 28th 1916

There have been two Zepp raids since last I wrote. One over Streatham last Saturday and on Monday a Zepp came down the Channel evidently on reconnoitering business. It approached Newhaven and dropped a flare outside the harbour. Then it sailed over the hills to Lewes and off behind Brighton before it took its departure. Of course we were plunged into darkness each night.

I've just returned from Newhaven by the mess car. At seven I discovered that the bus was discontinued. Racing over The Downs in the twilight – white cliffs and a sullen sea to the left – dark skies and rolling hills to the right – with a Tommie as chauffeur, I could only but be struck with the weird experiences of these times – when, oh when will they come to an end?

OCTOBER 4th 1916

And so another Night Duty has come to an end! 5pm will see me on duty in Brighton and Hove. How I enjoyed these last few nights in Kings. I've had varied staff nurses. Nurses F.L. Jones, Clifton, Waters and Atkins. F.L. Jones spoilt the men and gave hypodermic injections ad-lib. The next two were fearfully hard and Atkins proved a brick save that every second word approached a swear.

The men were bricks. Never shall I forget Dean and Metcalfe. Last night I left the tap running on the supper mugs in the kitchen sink. I entered the ward to help nurse and quite 15 minutes later I heard running water. I dashed to the kitchen but - bless you - 'twas inches under water and trays flowing round there in. Dean and Metcalfe were not in bed so I got them out to my aid and in no time the place was clear.

Then Gray was such a nice fellow. One day I thanked him for washing up the breakfast things and he replied: *"Hospital is the one place where we are thanked for what we do."*

Poor little Hutts was a V.D.H. case and in a serious condition but always so grateful for the slightest thing. Then Page – an acute appendix – was on 2 hourly salines while Galtereose – enemy gun shot wound – had an awful leg on continuous irrigation and woke the ward with his screams. Of course Evans considered himself fearfully ill thou his leg was nothing much. He would remind us every now and then that he was *"responsible for seven children"*!

I really must get to sleep – it is 1 o'clock.

OCTOBER 8th 1916

Yesterday, my first half day for two months, was spent at Newhaven. I had tea in Robin's hut with Collins and his mother. Such a storm was raging – a wild Sou' Wester blew straight across The Downs, lashing the sea into a perfect fury – so that down by the break water it seemed as thou angry demons were leaping the lighthouse with long lean arms outstretched.

Today I lunched with the Lowers. Colonel Lowers was present – likewise another Lt. Colonel and two other officers.

I must now to bed. Lights are just going out and I'm dead tired.

OCTOBER 10th 1916

Such a topping tea Evans, Page and I had this afternoon – in Evan's room – Page's brother supplied cream by post and we'd a regular feast between that and bananas.

Yesterday I spent the afternoon at Lewes with Whittle as my companion.

Sgt Parker has been awarded 1st prize in 'Blighty' for this poem:

THE DREAM RIDES

Good-day, miss! Pleased to see you; sit ye down aside the bed,
Yes. I'm feelin' pretty cushy – bar the noises in my head.
My leg and arm is better – but my head ain't none too grand,
It's of that I wants to tell you 'cos I know you'll understand.

I daren't tell the sisters and the nurses, 'tho' they're kind,
Would never understand the thoughts as passes thro' my mind.
So I've waited till you came again because I know you are,
In sympathy with any man as drives a motor car.
Now afore the fightin' started I was chauffeur to old Brown,
In a village in the east of Kent, what's known as Arbledown.
'I wasn't no bloomin' road-'og but when 'e went for a ride –
'I was gapin' and admirin' of the bloomin' countryside.

But when the scrappin' started, I took my bloomin' chance,
And 'listed as a driver for the A.S.C. in France:
And that is 'ow it comes about, a peaceful chap like me
Lies 'ere with bits of Krapsses in 'is arms, and 'ead and knee.

Now I was reared in London, and when first at 'Arbledown,
Was always longin' for the noise and traffic of a town.
But, 'fore I'd drove there very long, I soon began to feel,
That trees and grass and corn fields give a pleasure that is real.
Excuse me if I'm makin' this 'ere talk of mine too long,
My thoughts fair runs away with me, their steerin' gear goes wrong.
But what I wants to tell you, for I feel as 'ow I must,
Was the tricks my bloomin' noddle played the nights I lay 'ere just.
Now as I've got a busted leg, this arch, as p'raps you knows,
Is what they call a cradle, to 'old up the bloomin' clothes.

And as I looks, I gits at it (you can see from where you are),
It looks like nothin' 'arf so much as the bonnet of a car.
Now the first night as I was 'ere. I couldn't sleep a wink,
And tho' they made me cushy – I could do nought else but think.
And as I lay there a thinkin', I dropped into a doze,
With one bloomin' eyes arf open looking down the bloomin' clothes.
And as I lay there a lookin', for I knows where I are,
I was back again in Faney in Browny's bloomin' car.
Until one night I dropped right off and then I goes and dreams,
I'm drivin' over there in France towards the gunfire's gleams.
Back on my bloomin' lovy, my good old mandalay pet,
A peltin' on them awful roads, thro' all the mud and wet.

With my eyes a bulgin' from my 'ead for fear o' losin' sight,
Of the tail lamp of the man in front a slippin' thro' the night.
A 'eavy 'it the car in front and laid me in a 'eap,
With the driver and 'is mate stretched out in everlastin' sleep.
It shook my bus completely and I've no chance to stop,
And 'fore the flash 'ad died away she piled 'erself on top.
And then another bloomin' shell fair finished up the job,
And in a second I was 'ere, awake, so 'elp my God.
With the cradle and my busted leg a-layin' on the bed,
And the sound of Fritz's 'eavies a wringin' in my bloomin' 'ead.

I didn't want that dream again – so first thing the next day,
I tried to get the nurse to take that cradle thing away.
She asked me what the reason was, but 'er I wouldn't tell,
'Cos I knew that if I waited, you would understand me well.
I've seen you drive by in your car and knew that you would see,
The way that I was feelin' – a rough chauffeur chap like me.

Now you must be a goin', miss – the teas a comin' in,
But don't forget that Sunday's the next day for visitin'!

Written by J.R. Parker

THE V.A.D.'S "IF"
with apologies to Rudyard Kipling

If you can rush about all day and not feel tired,
Or, if you're fagged, can make them think your not.
By keeping up a smile, like one inspired,
And always being "Johnny-on-the-spot".
If you can so soothe the nasty, fretful patients,
What time your head is aching fit to split.
And not show signs of petulant impatience,
When other nurses ease their minds a bit.

If you can help a staff nurse with a dressing,
And at the same time make some beds and dust.
If you can bow beneath "a left hand blessing",
When smart retorts feel as if come they must.
If you can do these few things I have mentioned,
And hosts of others – you know them and I don't.
If, after years your vein is unabated,
You'll be the perfect nurse (or else you won't).

J.R.Parker Sgt
(11th Suffolks)

OCTOBER 14th 1916

How quiet the dormitory is tonight. Mayston has gone on night – that is more than half the reason – again "Canada" has a day off. Pine is my next door neighbour now.

Stanford Road goes on as usual. Cpl Smith was on duty at the door tonight. He is an old friend from Dyke Road days and I slipped out to him with a mug of cocoa and a piece of bread and butter. Result: *"I hope you will soon be back in Dyke Road Nurse!"*

Staff Sgt Briggs is now in Stanford Road. I also knew him on night in Dyke Road.

I must get to bed or I'll be last up and I'll have to put the lights out. Goodnight!

OCTOBER 19th 1916

I'm in the Officers Quarters and I'm having the time of my life just! Last Saturday I was hastily ordered from Stanford Road – the third time I have left that abode. Curiously enough I have never stayed there longer than a week!

Everyone expressed astonishment at my new abode – I'm said to be much too young and pretty! Something to console me in my old age. The men are perfectly topping. Before lights go out, let me mention a few.....

First and foremost there's Mr Rich – I must put him first because he's an awful terror and spends his time winking hard at me. This afternoon he never came in to tea – I asked him to explain his conduct and he replied that he never spoke to a girl since he couldn't have me with him!

Last night we'd a great concert and I found myself seated by his side. He expressed great delight and I felt the eyes of Matron and Divers Sisters fixed upon me. True, Sister Smith had ordered me to entertain the society but I think she considered matters were going too far. She came and seated herself between the two of us!

OCTOBER 20th 1916

Light went out in the midst of last night's account.

I'd a terrible time tonight. The Canadian, Mr Ritchie, volunteered to see me into the tram and I couldn't get rid of him – so I walked into the Nurse's room where Nurse Lockhead explained the situation to him.

We have two Mr Ritchies. The other is a tall striking looking Scots Guardsman. He's very quiet but such a nice chap – I'm very nearly in love with him!

COMPLIMENTS OF
PTE. E. CROSSLEY, N. STAFFS.

PEOPLE I REMEMBER STILL
"The Hospital Matron."

OCTOBER 21st 1916

I continue – seated on my bed.

I've been strafed this afternoon. I wore blue clock stockings and suede shoes! Quite fetching! Tommie was fearfully perturbed – she must be jealous!! Anyhow, my shoes have turned up from the bootmakers so she'll be relieved to see me in other footwear tomorrow. All the same I must stick to the stockings.

I'll get the sack from my present abode if Mr Rich keeps up his present behaviour. He is not a Canadian but a Londoner aged 27. He has had his foot amputated and he is a caution. I told him he was spoilt where upon he replied that the one thing spoilt about him was his looks! Certainly he is not beautiful but he has such a cheeky cheeky face – I fear he is quite my favourite. Of course he can't talk to one without winking. I tell him he's a sinner but it's no good.

Tonight he met me on the stairs and as he hobbled by on crutches he queried as to whether I was aware of the fact that he loved me!! I felt like saying he'd better keep quiet about it or I'd be sent on a long holiday! But he immediately made off – I fear he's a sad flirt. By the way, I find this is the second note concerning Mr Rich so I'd better get a move on – then there's Mr Laurie poor old chap – over six foot two in height, he has a fearful leg and arm – he will only limp through life from now on – he is a Scot and hails from Selkirk.

Lights are going out goodnight.

Riverside House
Bandon
Co. Cork

Dear Nurse Pulvertaft –

Your surmise was correct, namely that I did wonder who the letter was from. I could see it was not from Lieut. Glanville as the handwriting had a distinctly feminine touch. By the way, is it that young Irishman to whom you have given the name Redmond?

I asked him how Carson was doing, but he has not yet replied. I shouldn't be surprised to learn that instead of writing to me he indulges in chats with you. And I'm sure I for one, don't blame him! Therefore, by all the laws of Euclid and such-like tormentors of humanity, you will – but – I forgot a girl does not believe in that sort of logic, anyway – you will, of course, write to me soon again and make up for that miscreants delinquencies.

You write such a splendid letter that I shall only ask you to continue "Comme ça" or "Comme vous voulez".

You will excuse my wonderful flow of French I hope – the result of spending the best year or more of my life on the Continent.

I hope to be in Skibbereen before long and I shall give it my love for you. Yes, I shall give it my love because it is such a lonely place. Shall matron if fine, will you come? Jolly nice to go on then to Glengarriff and round by the lakes.

Can you quite imagine the ward below being a handful to manage, but I guess it will be done; even without Matron. How are all the Sisters, especially Sister Shannon and Sister Smith? Any chap who gets sent to the hospital on Doyle Road must have been born under a lucky star.

Hope you are enjoying life at the officers quarters now. Did we really look such frights? Sorry, very sorry, don't you know but frights will be frights. I suppose the girls will be but — Irish. I assure you I am most thoroughly Irish, but, for all that, a true Imperialist. And God helping, Britons never shall be slaves!!! I'd rather wish you had as much of an Irish accent as I have! I love it!!!

I am yrs. Very sincerely,
Capt. P.L.G. Bennett.

Dear Compatriot, Nurse Grace

I really don't suppose you are still at No. 2 Eastern, but anyway I can't convey my best wishes for the new year to you unless I try some address. And it would never do to pretend to forget you when I most certainly don't.

You may by this time have come to France; if so perchance we may again meet out here.

Though it's also possible — accuracy might demand the word "probably" in the superlative value — that you may be married by now, in which case (no matter how many hospitals I pass through) the likelihood of meeting you out here would, I suppose, be ended? You are still, I hope, not ashamed to own yourself Irish, are you?

Give my kind regards and best wishes to the L.B.E.W. If you are near it please. Do you still stay at the Sacred Heart? Am with an Ambulance — the C.2 Field Ambulance — since return to France. I had a couple of months in Old Ireland before returning here, so I didn't do too badly. Spent quite a time in one of the cities on the River Lee.

The weather is absolutely fantastic at present. The ground is said to be so hard that a 17 inch shell only penetrates an inch or two. I don't say the rumour is quite accurate! Possibly they sit a bit deeper than that.

Hope you are not being bombed, wherever you are.

Yours gratefully,
Capt. P. Bennett

OCTOBER 24th 1916

We had another concert last night. Cpt Bate sang a verse concerning 'blue eyes' as an encore – I was in the line of fire and he nodded at me as he reached the closing bars. I've heard of it since! I'm told I ought to wear goggles when I go out etc. etc.

This afternoon I had tea at Clarks with Bennet and her mother – I'm managing to enjoy life these days!

This is one of the many notes written by Mr Watt – suffering from shell shock – before he recovered his speech.

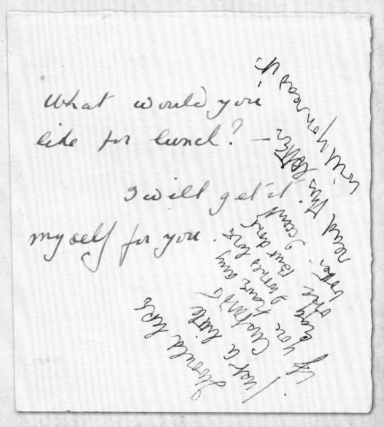

OCTOBER 29th 1916

I'd an evening off this Sunday so I'm early in bed. Quite a change for me – I've horrible threatings of a toothache but we'll hope for the best. This afternoon I'd my photo taken by Mr Skull and Mr Rich. Babington and I were on alone and 'twas difficult enough to keep one eye on the camera and the other on the door lest Matron should be lurking round. Good night now – I'm sleepy.

NOVEMBER 1st 1916

Mr Williamson sent me home tonight – no cause for alarm. Sister chaperoned me. Capt Bennett wrote to Mr Glanville a short while back: *"Take care of your heart – it's a bad thing if that goes wrong. For further information concerning this malady apply to Sister Shannon or N. Pulvertaft!"*

Whittle o.a.s. France.

Whittle has just been asked to go abroad – I hope this keeps her out of a convent.

Wedekind is seriously ill in the Sussex County.

Myself snapped in Gordon by **Mr Skull**.

NOVEMBER 2nd 1916

I've left my officers. I'm sad and yet I'm glad. Tomorrow will see me in Kings once more – with Newton – who is considered my double!

My officers were most flatteringly sad at my departure. Mr Laurie said he would certainly have a relapse. Mr Richie considered it exceedingly wrong of me to leave Mr Claponan in his serious condition – the latter had his op. today.

As I passed the mess door there was a regular cry of dismay – Mr Fortier and Mr Skull demanded an immediate explanation and I referred them to Matron. The former went out directly after dinner, his parting shot was *"Sister Pulvertaft – Where's my stud, my pipe, my collar and my tie pin?"* Such a nice fellow as he was! But he would insist that I lost everything when I tided his locker.

Mr Rich has promised me Divers snaps and a billet duex. Hope they arrive.

Bennet and I had tea on the pier and forgot today!

NOVEMBER 11th 1916

Yesterday Newton had her day off and I had the morning. We went down on the West Pier and ran into "Block B". Messers - Clapman - Watt - Fortier - Skull - Barker - Granville - Cole. I was snapped by Mr Skull whilst conversing with Mr Barker. At 6.30pm I was once again summoned from Kings to the officer's quarters – a convoy had arrived and Sister Smith borrowed me. She was most flattering and expressed a desire that I might remain with her but *"Matron considers you too useful"* was her flattering remark.

The men seemed quite pleased to see me once more, Mr Fortier wished to know my hours on the pier! I could not give them so he said he must spend every morning down there!

This was the second time I had left Kings since starting my work there. The first time I went over to Block B with Lolly once again by Sister Smith's request. Poor Kiddie – he died of tetanus the same night – I saw the lumbar puncture performed.

Mrs Green "Charlady"
(Lincoln & Gordon).

Not long back, I ran into Redmond and Carson on the look out for Nurse Shannon – the night nurse – I guessed she'd overslept herself as 'twas strictly against rules for the night nurse to get up so early – accordingly I went back to the convent and called her. I then met Redmond and Carson once more and taxied as far as the dials with them and Mr Glanville then insisted on paying my full fare. I met a Mr Twig last night who knows Isney of Dungannon etc.

Tents of Block B.

Outside Block B.
Messers. Skull. Brigden. Ritchie. Chapman.
Williamson. Cole. Norman. Barker. Horstall.

NOVEMBER 13th 1916

Once more I've been summoned to the officers quarters – a special was needed yesterday afternoon and I spent my time in Kelvin. Now Newton has gone on night and I am the one V.A.D. in Kings.

NOVEMBER 16th 1916

A French Canadian was admitted last night. I was off duty this morning and this afternoon noticed that he lay in bed without speaking a word.

So hearing he spoke French I tried my hand – true enough – he immediately opened conversation and Waters – an Irishman next door – made this remark: *"Trust sweet Dublin, you can speak to him tho' the Colonel could not make him understand a word this morning."*

DECEMBER 2nd 1916

I'll turn Christian Scientist after today. This morning I'd a raking headache and felt horribly groggy. I spent the afternoon in my bed and went on duty at 5pm feeling decidedly wobbly, only to discover that two cases had come in for immediate operation. I had to escort them to the theatre and did so in fear and trembling – but all went well and in a miraculous manner my head had disappeared.

Given to me by a patient in Kings Ward......

Foreword
By the Rev. Canon F.J. Meyrick, M.A.
St. Peter Mancroft Vicarage, Norwich

MANY an anxious parent is seeing visions by day and dreaming dreams by night. Often the vision or the dream is a horror, haunting and terrible. Often, thank God, it is something very lovely and full of comfort.

Many of us, whose dear ones are, by day and night, flung into the midst of so many and great dangers, will be reminded by this dream of the great spiritual Forces, who, acting for God, become a boy's shield and buckler in the hour of battle.

God, the Father of us all, wishes to do the best, the very best, for all His sons. Even if He asks His son "to leap the golden stile," it does not mean that the mother's prayer or the child's prayer has been unheard. On the other hand, who can measure the power of prayer in protecting those who are dear? Prayer is the appeal of love to Love for a loved one.

How beautiful it is to see little children trooping into Church and quietly kneeling in a "War Corner." These children love their "Daddies," and they know God loves them, so they just say, "Please God, take care of Daddy" – love appealing to Love for a loved one.

And if the mother's beautiful dream is a comfort and an inspiration, it is also a rebuke. Those dear boys in the firing line are doing their bit for me and for my home. What am I doing for them? Perhaps I cannot do much, but I may ask God to keep them very near to Him. I may ask Him, if it be His will, to bring them home again. I may ask Him, I must ask Him, that when peace comes, those who survive may return home to an England that is worthy of the men whose lives have been so gloriously offered, and of the women who have so cheerfully, even proudly, endured the heart ache, who in some cases, have received wounds which time will never heal.

Read the mother's beautiful dream. Pray for all who are anxious and bereaved. Pray for the sailor and the soldier. Pray for our English homes. Don't let the protecting "Prayer Shadows fade away."

Originally printed by Jarrold and Sons Publishers, London and Norwich.

THE TWELVE O'CLOCK WAR BELL – A DREAM OF THE TRENCHES

I HAD gone to sleep full of thoughts of the war, for my boy was in the trenches in France, and was rarely out of my mind, and this beautiful dream came to me, and has been a great help ever since.

In my dream I was in France, with some one at my side, who seemed both companion and guide, although I never saw who it was all the time, and do not even know if it was a man or a woman. We seemed passing through the air, and it was misty all around, so that I saw nothing although I was conscious of it being another country. Suddenly my companion said in a quiet voice *"There are the trenches"* and I found that the mist was gone, and that just before, and rather below us, were the very lines of trenches that we had pictured to ourselves so often of late.

Yes: there they were, and the men were in them, waiting and watching, while guns were firing and shells bursting all around. A great horror and pity took possession of me, as I saw all these young bright lives in deadly peril, and I was filled with a great longing to do something to protect them from these terrible dangers. Just then I saw what I had not noticed before, that all along the parapet of the trenches was a long line of shadowy figures, that sometimes seemed to be actual men and women, and sometimes merely shadows or mist forms. In front of some of the men were many more than others, but all had some, and I distinctly knew that they were protecting the men from the dangers all around them, although they seemed so dream-like and unsubstantial.

"What are those shadows in front of the men?" I cried to my companion, and I knew what the answer would be before it came. *"They are the prayers of those at home."* was the reply, and I felt a thrill of joy and shame, for how few and weak had been my prayers, and yet they meant so much.

We stayed a long time, and to my grief and pain I saw that the line of Prayer Shadows was fading away, and in some places the men were left without any protection at all.

"What can we do?" I cried; *"Is no one praying at home?"* But at that moment there seemed to be a movement in the air, and a slight rushing sound coming nearer and nearer, and my companion spoke softly and yet with a tone of intense relief *"It is 12 o'clock and the children are coming."* and hosts and hosts of little shadowy forms came from everywhere, and the line in front of the trenches was thicker than before, and the men were protected again! The relief was intense, and I woke.

. . . .

A Mother.

10.12.16

Dear Nurse Pulvertaft

I am writing to you for my husband, who just at the present is unable to use his right hand owing to a dog having bit his fore-finger quite recently.

But owing to him receiving this photograph lately, he was anxious for you to have a copy to add to your collection. Thanking you for your care and attention to him whilst in your charge. Of which he has often spoke of to me.

He is now able to get about well, considering his wound and just at present is classed in category C.3.P. with a little light employment.

Yours sincerely

Florence Vardy.

DECEMBER 12ᵗʰ 1916

I've just returned from dinner with the Hills – roast chicken, sausages, bread sauce, potatoes, turnips, apple tart, cheese and dessert. A sumptuous repast after convent fare! I had a military escort back here – Hill's butler seeing me as far as the convent. Hill is the afternoon helper in Kings and an exceedingly nice girl.

It's after 10 – Goodnight.

DECEMBER 24ᵗʰ 1916

It is Christmas Eve and I must add a line for that reason alone – all I can say is I have never yet spent it in a convent and I sincerely hope I shall never get the chance of spending it there again. Somehow it makes me think of Scrooge in a Christmas Carol.

Convoy tonight so I must get a move on.

Christmas Card - Sgt & Mrs Vardy.

DECEMBER 25th 1916 – CHRISTMAS DAY!

My first Christmas away from home has come to an end and I am not sorry! True it has been extraordinarily happy but yet there has been a feeling of sadness present all day long – or so it has seemed to me.

At 5am I was awakened by Whittle and went to early service at 6 – it was pitch dark and raining fast. Walking to chapel with my Christmas breakfast of bread and butter in my hand – the great comparison between this Christmas and all the others I have spent was most forcibly brought before me. In normal time 5.45am would have found me in bed and not stumbling down a slippery road in inky darkness, while breakfast would hardly have consisted of a piece of bread and a cup of tea snatched between bed making! But there's a war on and it makes a difference!

Nurse Shannon and I soon got through that breakfast but we looked into the ward first. Strains of mouth organs and tin whistles – sad to relate – have been wafting into chapel – I put it down to the orderlies – but no! Kings was to blame. As we entered the ward at 6.45am such a welcome greeted us – whistles, rattles and pipes sounded on all sides while the latest rag time was rattled off from the platform, Sgt Barton being the pianist. Dearle was there – of course – he being an artiste as far as mouth organs were concerned and it was with difficulty we tore ourselves from the scene.

Needless to say, dressings were hurried through in a truly remarkable manner. Then the Colonel arrived and Carter the A.D.M.S. – the Colonel to shake hands with each man in turn, wishing them all that was good – the A.D.M.S. to read a letter from his majesty, the King. All this time a quaint couple were parading the ward – Sgt Barton and Metcalfe – Surgeon and V.A.D. They created great amusement, behaving in a truly absurd manner and time passed quickly until dinner hour – such a table as was spread – sweets of every kind – plum pudding, of course, and a turkey carved by Major Ionides. Dinners were served round to bed patients first, but they refused to start off straight away. *"We have not said grace yet!"* was Taffy's remark – commonly known as Private Jones.

After dinner we received each wards decorations in turn and then came tea, the evening work and then we raced back to our Christmas dinner – roast beef (barely warm – for dressings were heavy and we were late), then plum pudding. Matron next gave each nurse a memento from Miss Ionides.

We were thankful to get to bed. Don't think I missed my Christmas Turkey entirely – Shankie had a day off and went home – she returned with turkey and sausage in a paper bag and Tommie and I shared it, seated on my bed and eating it with fingers as forks. So Christmas 1916 came to an end.

All Glory be to God on High, And to the Earth be Peace. Goodwill henceforth from Heaven to Men. Begin and never cease.

Christmas Card - Matron.

Nº 36. GENERAL HOSPITAL

ATTACHED

ROYAL SERBIAN ARMY

With best wishes

FROM

M Lunt

CHRISTMAS 1916.

DECEMBER 31st 1916

1915 and 1916 have found me as a V.A.D. in hospital
– may 1917 find me with "my civy clothes on".

Words copied from Christmas card of the 2nd Rhodesia
Regt. E. Africa 1916:

We Rhodesians send you greetings,
From this dusty torrid zone.
And we drink to merry meeting,
In that pleasant place called "home".
Wasting war won't last for ever,
Fleeing Hun must come to bay.
Friends ——— relations here together.
Wish you peace this Christmas day.

GERARD & MARIN   PARIS

106-A

Virgin, Infant Jesus and Saint John
(of Botticelli).

The Convent Christmas Card.

XMAS 19__ AT ____ HOS___ BRIGHTON.
(WILES. HOVE.)
No 33.

The Four Seasons

The art of the Christmas decorator, found in every ward of the many buildings, reached its highest expression in the King's Ward at the Dyke-road Hospital. This nobly-proportioned and handsomely-appointed hall had been made to present a charming scene of "floral" beauty. By the use of a large number of paper flowers, made by wounded men, it was found possible to carry out an elaborate scheme of floral decorations representing "The Four Seasons." For "Spring" one corner of the hall seemed full of light pink snow, made by the apple blossom starring widely spread branches. A patch of tulips made vivid colour below. "Summer" was secured in the most effective manner by transforming the platform into an old-world garden. Its steps and railings lend themselves admirably to the suggestion of garden terraces and balustrading. Here were arbours of roses and climbing flowers, parterres of vivid blossoms, shrubberies and miniature avenues, all laid out, not merely in haphazard fashion, but with the eye of a landscape gardener seeking picturesque effect. A moss-covered sundial supplied the element of romance. "Autumn" was secured by means of trees laden with fruit and some handsome chrysanthemums, glowing amber and red. "Winter" had a very cheering Christmas-tree effect, with a considerable space filled by spreading boughs glittering with silver hoar-frost. In the snow-bound ground from which these trees grew, one could trace the design of trenches, while at a miniature dug-out a sentry stood on guard. Over the nurses' table spread an arbour of roses, framing the inscription, "A Merry Xmas to Sister and Nurses." This was a little surprise the men sprang on the nurses. The arches of the upper part of the hall were outlined with holly and paper flowers, and every suitable spot was decorated. A finishing touch was secured by covering the electric lights with transparencies so designed as to produce the effect of the air being haunted by luminous owls. In themselves they were the quaintest of birds. But an additional value was the softening and toning of the light, so that the whole picturesque scheme was invested with a mellow glamour. One could only hope that actual pain was wiled away as the appearance of it was thus taken away from the beds and their occupants.

Every ward was decorated with green, with flowers, and with mottoes. Some of them suggested an arrested snowstorm, with the air full of flakes; one, by the way of contrast, aimed at an orange grove, with the branches full of yellow balls, in some cases the real fruit being used. Individual taste was allowed a free hand, and designs, curious or elegant, figured on many a wall.

WINTER - and dinner time!
Serles, Sister Farren, Barr, Parks, Miss Ellis.

SPRING: Myself, Mayhew (Trenchfoot), Johnson (Appendix), Paget (Haematemesis).

XMAS 1916 AT DYKE RD HOS

SUMMER: Sparrow, Dunstan, Biggens, Winston, Barr, Miss Ellis, Nurse Shannon, Sister Farren, Myself, Nurse Jones, Lawrence, Bantin, Jones, McLean, Lindley, Metcalfe, Holt, Price, Potter, Henderson – "The Balmoral".

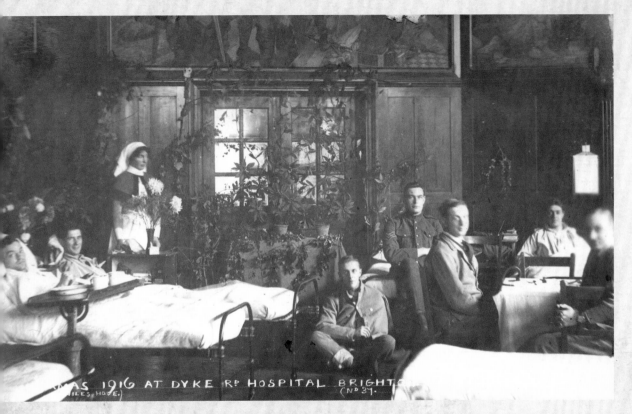

XMAS 1916 AT DYKE RD HOSPITAL BRIGHTON (No 37.)

AUTUMN: Atudworth, Sturman, Nurse Shannon, Winson, Serles, Sparrow, Sullivan, Price.

Surgeon Sergt. Bantin
and Nurse Metcalfe.
Snapped by Nurse
Turner – Christmas 1916.

Bugler J. Parker,
830254.

90th Little Black Devil's,
Winnipeg.

Cpl Morton – York Ward.

"Mummy's Pet"
Pte Lancer – York Ward

139.

JANUARY 7th 1917 – SUNDAY NIGHT

'Tis difficult indeed to get a line written tonight. Tommy and Trask have just raided the dormitory. They persisted that 'twas untidy and made a dash for the top where Shankie was endeavouring to make her bed. A pillow fight ensued and peace seems far off. I've just had supper – Penie brought hot coffee up to my cubicle and we supped in state off that and cake. 'Tis an awful night – pouring rain outside.

We gave two great entertainments this Christmas – one to the staff – the other to the lady Chars. First of all came a sketch "Between the Soup and the Savoury". I acted parlour maid, Shankie kitchen maid and Mrs Fizpatrick, cook. Then a few tableaux followed after which a group of Gypsy Parrots performed. It went off quite well. The second night the entertainment was given in the Sgt mess room – all peep holes were carefully screened or so Matron thought – but such indeed was not the case. The R.A.M.C. seemed to know a lot about everything the next morning and it seems that quite a crowd viewed proceedings through a chink in the window blinds.

This is the first Sunday in 1917 and the last for many a V.A.D. here. Guy, Evans, Williams, Lock and Tower – what will they be doing next Sunday? I wonder!

A RED CROSS NURSE

The little sinner "Oh Hamb..."

140.

THE OPENING CHORUS OF OUR GYPSY PARROT TROUPE TO THE TUNE OF TIPPERARY AT THE CHRISTMAS ENTERTAINMENT 1916

Christmas time has come again and let's be glad and gay,
Forget your troubles, worries, cares and join with us today.
Sing aloud a merry ditty, crack a cheery joke,
And lets forget we ever felt like piggies in a poke.

We're a merry little troupe of gypsy parrots,
And we've come to cheer your hearts.
Remember it's our first appearance,
So it's not so bad for a start - eh?
If you will kindly listen to us,
Our frolics jokes and songs.
Then life to you will seem a little brighter,
You'll forget your woes and wrongs.

Nursing is an arduous job, our tempers suffer sore,
We get fed up and tired and cross and wish we were no more.
But we must just remember there are others too today,
Who likewise feel fed up and cross so let's join hands and say –

It's a poor heart that ne'er rejoices,
Let come what may –
The boys have done their best for England,
And its up to us today –
To give them a smile and cheery welcome,
And make their wards like home.
For be they English or Colonial,
Their British to the backbone.

VALE BY SISTER DRAPER

Written for the V.A.D.s who left Jan: 10th 1917 and sung to the tune of - John Brown's Body at the Christmas Entertainment 1916.

Farewell Sisters – but we go our separate ways,
Goodbye to Brighton and all its muddled days.
Change of scene is good for all and change of method pays –
So now we're packing up to go.

Goodbye Tippets who have helped us all the while,
Backed us up with friendliness and cheered us with a smile –
Doubt not that we shall miss you as we tread the lonely mile,
For now we're packing up to go.

V.A.D.s goodbye to you and always wish you luck –
Tho' they hurry you from ward to ward they still admire your pluck –
Many a time no doubt you all wishing you could chuck,
Some day you'll be packing up to go.

Orderlies good day to you! They've tried to teach you some –
What tho they stopped your weekly pass and left you looking glum –
No doubt you took it out some how and made the barracks hum –
Pray why don't you pack up and go?

A word to those who follow us – don't worry over much,
It's a very strenuous struggle but there's still the funny touch –
If red tape trips you everywhere – just swear in double dutch –
Then you'll be packing up to go!

Matron we bow to you – We've asked you here tonight –
So lay aside your worries and we'll sing with all our might.
One little word we leave with you before we say goodnight –
Don't you start packing up to go!

Sep 17/16

Sergeant Major Hall

The General Officer Comd
Commanding the 24th Div. would
be glad if you could supply

five good men to go up to

the Hospital & lift him out of

bed to enable him to inspect

the troops the time stated is

2 PM sharp. please reply

at ... Workhouse for

Field Marshal Paul Lawrence K.C.B
M.V.O. M.I.C.E. K.C.M.G. C.B. W.C.

143.

JANUARY 15th 1917

I write in our new sitting room – we have exchanged with the Terriers – they have our great barn and we have this cosy little room – with five comfy wicker and hammock chairs supplied by Divers people – Miss Ionides sent two. I have been sewing hard and also adding to this book. I go home on the 12th June for three months and would like to finish the book by then if possible.

Nurse F. L. Jones has Diphtheria and is now in the Sanatorium. Martin returned from three months holidays only to develop measles the next day – so she has likewise taken her departure.

Poor Hicks died the other day – never did I feel so terribly sorry – he was not on my side in Kings but I would constantly meet him out with his wife for he was only married a year – he had a gun shot wound to his arm and a week ago he was brought into theatre and some dead bone was removed. I accompanied him and the whole thing took about two minutes – a whiff of gas being used. Evidently a lot of blood was dislodged and it went to his brain. Four days afterwards he died – Sic transit gloria mundi.

JANUARY 17th 1917

A morning off today. There's snow on the ground and as the nuns are clearing out the dormitory I have come down to this sitting room to write letters. I forgot my watch and went back to the dormitory saying to the little French nun as I passed *"I've never yet remembered to bring everything down with me."*

"Quand on n'a pas de tete - on doit avoir des jambes" – was her reply.

[*"When one has no head - one must have legs."*]

144.

JANUARY 18ᵗʰ 1917

The news is out – Capt. Bell and Sister Smith are engaged. The former I knew well as an officer patient in B Block – but fancy Sister Smith setting such an example ————— Well !

These are Lawrence's epistles. Lawrence has a fractured femur – He is not on my side of the ward but has an idea that I can supply the wants of the entire ward. Hence he always applies to me for everything.

Handed to me with two hot water bottles!

Nurse Pulvertaft

With the Generals compliments and he hopes you will grant him this favour.

Field Marshall Earl Lawrence, K.C., M.V.G., L.R.A.M., F.R.C.D., L.D.S., M.R.C.P., F.R.C.S. etc. etc.

Camp's Headquarters

The General desires to express his gratitude for the smartness in which way you fulfil your duties, as hot water bottle attendant and he has also recommended you to be decorated with the order of the "De La Hot Water Bottle."

Field Marshall Earl Lawrence, K.C., M.V.G., L.R.A.M., F.R.C.D., L.D.S., M.R.C.P. etc. etc. etc.

JANUARY 21st 1917

Today I've been decorated with the one medal I shall ever receive – at 12.30 prompt. I paraded before Field Marshall Earl Lawrence to receive the order of *de la hot water Bottle*.

Nurse Pulvertaft

You are to parade at 2:30pm in the Kings Ward to receive the Decoration which has been granted.

Dress: Slacks
Shoes: Brown
Blouse: Low Neck (and very low)
Stockings: Transparent

No frills must not be showing until after the Decoration.

By order of General Lawrence K.C. etc.

The General cannot accept such terms and he desires to know for why a Secretary should dictate to a General as to what dress should be worn. When the General orders a certain dress this dress must be worn.

THE JOYS OF A GENERAL HOSPITAL.

EVENTS THAT LEND VARIETY TO THE MONOTONOUS EXISTENCE OF OUR WOUNDED WARRIORS.

"V.A.D."

We in the busy ward
Stay not to dream; for God has closed our eyes
Lest, fronted by your giant sacrifice,
O brothers maimed and pale,
The hearts that see to serve you, faint and fail!

We, handmaids of your pain, pass onward
And speak not of your glory; God has hung
His silence on our lips, lest praises sung
Scare your mirth-makings,
And break your happy talk of trivial things.

This be our sacrifice,
You who have given all for one great Dream!
Steadfast enduring at the sober task
Of days and nights that seem
Grey-winged and glamourless – we will not ask
For flashing visions of an earlier day;
And – if it serve you, brothers – dreamless be our way!

Hither have brought us
Those years wherein we chased the flying moon,
Sought the blue roses, sailed the seas of June-
Into this quiet shade
Where Vision sleeps, and Youth to rest is laid.
Through song and laughter, through the woods of Spring
(Our youth had taught us)
We came with dancing step and lute playing
Most tender-sweet,
Only for this – to kneel and wash your feet.

O Sacrament unguessed beside the lowly bed!
Not you, not you alone
Wait on our care. Perchance there waiteth One
(And yet we cannot see)
Who for our sake hath walked among the dead;
Whose Feet His daughters wash, as once in Bethany.
Yet, if He will,
His Hand be on our eyes, that we go sightless still.

Mary-Adair MacDonald

BACK TO LONDON – OCTOBER 1917

St Gabriel's College. (1st London General Hospital, R.A.M.C.(T) Myatt Par[k]

OCTOBER 11th 1917

After many months! These entries will concern my half day work at the 1st London General, Camberwell.

Behold me in Ward 34 – Officers – charging up and down a seemingly endless ward with trays most of the time. My hours are as follows: Mondays, Wednesdays and Fridays 2 – 7.30, Sundays, Tuesdays, Thursdays and Saturdays 8.30 – 1.15.

I only started this week so there is little to record. For the first time I'm working in a hut. After Brighton the ward seems horribly untidy. The beds are a perfect disgrace. But then officers are ——— !

Two nice Canadians left today – they looked me up in the pantry to say goodbye. The one remarked: *"Sorry you've not been longer on our ward, nurse."* The other: *"Take care of the officers – they need some looking after."*

"Is this right for 'eadquarters?" "Yes, change at Oxford Circus."

BRITISH RED CROSS SOCIETY.

STREATHAM DIVISION

STANDING ORDERS.

1.—Uniform Certificates must be returned to me for endorsement, without fail, on the expiration of six months from the date of issue. Owing to postal risks it is preferable that Members should bring them to me in person for signature.

2.—Change of Name or Address must be notified me at once.

3.—Temporary leave of absence from home must be applied for in writing. The temporary address and the period of leave required must be stated.

4.—A regular monthly Postcard must be sent me on the 20th day of each month stating the duty in which you have been employed and the hours daily you have given.

5.—Personal applications to Hospitals for work is not allowed. Members desiring work, or change of work, must apply for it through me. A letter from a Matron asking for a particular Member is always considered as also are the wishes of a Member to be posted to a particular Hospital.

6.—The following Drills, Meetings and Parades are compulsory, unless a valid excuse in writing is sent to me beforehand.

 a—MONTHLY MEETING, 8 p.m. the 1st Saturday, in every month.

 b—CHURCH PARADE, 2nd Sunday in every month, parade at St. Leonard's Hall, 10.40 a.m.

 c—DRILL, Thursday 7.45 p.m. Twelve Divisional Drills at least must be attended during the year to retain Membership in the Detachment. Recruits must attend drill every week for the first three months.

7.—First Aid and Home Nursing Certificates must be obtained by all Members of the Detachment within a year of date of enrolment. A full years service in a Hospital exempts a Member from one examination and entitles her to an Exemption Certificate. This also applies to a Member who is already in possession of one Certificate and a similiar service entitles her to her Advanced Certificate.

8.—UNIFORM Remember that you are wearing the King's uniform, and that it must be worn correctly and smartly.

 Hats, not caps, must always be worn on Parade.

 Aprons must not be worn underneath the long coat.

 Grey Gloves are not to be worn on Parade, always white.

 Shoes, Stockings and Spats must be black. High-heeled shoes, or shoes with buckles, are not to be worn.

 Jewellery must never be worn.

 Scarves may be worn, but must be white, blue or black.

 Furs or Veils must never be worn.

 An Umbrella must never be carried.

 Special Service Probationers and General Service Members must wear the Badges designed for them on the left forearm of their coat sleeve. General Service Members must also wear the brown shoulder straps. Keep your hair tidy, and do not use powder, paint or scent. Keep your clothes well brushed, and your shoulder titles well polished. Smoking in public places is strictly prohibited. On leaving my Detachment, all Badges, Buttons and Shoulder Titles must be returned. If you wish to sell your Uniform, particulars should be sent to me.

Capt Angols &
V.A.D. Awdry

Sister Lacey.

?, Mr Jones and
V.A.D. Holmes.

Myself, snapped by
Mr Redshaw

Sister Atkins.

V.A.D. Pugh, Mr Jones
and T.P.Carter.

Sister Williams
& Mr Margetson.

Sister Lowe R.R.C.
Charge Sister.

V.A.D. Yetts and
Sister Haviland.

OCTOBER 15th 1917

Today I was reprimanded all round for entertaining a Charlie Chaplin in the kitchen. Not my fault – the Chaplain looked into the kitchen as he passed and enquired as to whether any of us were Irish. I proclaimed my nationality and he immediately became greatly interested – said he knew my brother – namely Pappy if you please.

OCTOBER 16th 1917

Today I learned that Mr Stranger came from Toronto. He dined with Dick Templeton and his wife the night before he sailed for England. Also it seems that my name was mentioned at mess and some officer announced that he knew my brothers well at Westminster School.

OCTOBER 18th 1917

Mr Wild left today. He told me to ask a "Miss Pulvertaft" living off the Western Road, Cork, as to whether she remembered S.M. Wild and a certain dance on St. Patrick's night 1915!!

Memorial Car
A gift from Mrs Slatter – lady cha

"Suffer little Children to come unto Me."

In Affectionate Rememberance

OF

THE POOR VICTIMS

Who lost their lives by Hostile Aircraft in the Raid on London

ON OCTOBER 19th, 1917.

"In the Midst of Life, We are in Death"

All tears are vain; we cannot now recall thee;
 Gone is thy loving voice and kindly face—
Gone from the home we so dearly loved thee;
 Where none can ever fill thy vacant place.
"There came a mist and a weeping rain,
 And life is never the same again."

Bargess, Printer, 8, York Place, Strand.

OCTOBER 29th 1917

Slid down in the ward today – tray in hand and was asked how I enjoyed the trip. Also fell out with Mr Stranger over Sinn Feiners and Ireland (separatists).

NOVEMBER 9th 1917

Tonight I was told there was a vacancy for an organist in Passchendale Church. Would I accept the offer!?

NOVEMBER 15th 1917

According to Lt. Brotherton, years ago, when I was quite a little child (!), the fairies flew down from the sun and kissed my hair e'er their return. Quite the most poetic compliment I have yet been paid!

Newspaper clippings – patients in Ward 34.

...YAL INVESTITURE.

...t. Whittington (left), M.C., and Capt. Staley, M.C.

SHOT IN THE TONGUE
Wounded Captain's Splendid Gallantry Though Jaw Was Broken.

"No praise can be too great for his splendid gallantry and devotion to duty."

This is the official comment on the conduct of Temporary Captain H. Driver, D.S.O. (Bedfords), who has just been awarded the Military Cross.

Fired at by snipers and machine guns, he showed not the slightest hesitation in continuing his rounds, even after he had been hit by a sniper, his jaw broken and his tongue shot.

T./Capt. HARRY DRIVER, D.S.O., Bed. R.- After gallantly leading his company in the attack, he successfully, and at great personal risk, so placed his advanced posts as to continually frustrate hostile counter-attacks. He repeatedly visited his posts under heavy and continuous shell fire, and personally directed the fire of his men. It was through his frequent and daring reconnaissances that the movements of the enemy troops were noticed and severely dealt with by our artillery on his information. Although fired at by snipers and machine-guns, he showed not the slightest hesitation in continuing his rounds from post to post, even after he had been hit by a sniper, his jaw broken, and his tongue shot through finally only giving up when suffering from loss of blood. Even then he wrote a full report of the situation, and stated to whom he was handing over his command. No praise can be too great for his splendid gallantry and devotion to duty.

154.

Myself, Mr Jones, Sister Wright
snapped by Holmes.

Padré Mackintosh.

Mr Jones, Sister Williams, Capt Argols.

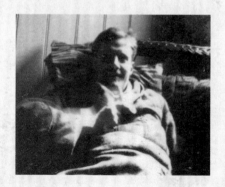

Capt Christie.

Capt Swan.

Capt Argols.

OVERNMENT
LADIES!

Mrs Macer &
Mrs Hancock,
Lady Chars,
Ward 34.

Primo Owen Pierce Jones R.A.O.B

156.

NOVEMBER 18th 1917

Thompson wrote Bryan (my brother) the
other day asking that I should look him up.
He heard I was working in Ward 34.
He himself is in Ward 35. Well I saw
him the other day and being formally
impressed I thought I'd drop in again today,
so I brought a large box of powder along
to beautify myself. Well, at the critical
moment the button came off my shoe and
having merely a safety pin to keep things
together I determined to defer my visit.

Some time later, toiling up Brixton Hill,
I heard a tommy's voice from the rear:
*"My! Nurse – if you waste anymore o' that
powder you'll have none left for your
massage in the morning!"*

For over a mile I'd been shedding a
pageant pink trail, the powder having
opened in my case!!

Mr Miller and Capt Thompson.

NOVEMBER 19th 1917

A voice came thro' the 'phone tonight: *"Is that you, Taffy?"* Imagine my surprise. However it was merely Captain Keith phoning the ward – "Pulvertaft" proved too much for his fractured jaw.

Tonight – to my great delight – I recognised a quotation from Tennyson, unknown to Mr Trail!

DECEMBER 7th 1917

During the raid that took place in the early hours of Dec 6th, two incoming bombs were dropped on the 1st London General. One outside Ward 35. The other outside 25. No damage was done. One bomb proved a dud, the other spent itself in the air.

My name has been made by my egg flips. Mr Butler sent Mr Bowen round the other day to enquire as to my method. I sent a bottle of vanilla back by return. Mr Butler and Mr Bowen are old patients from Ward 34 – they now dwell in the college. Today on my way to dinner I was captured by the latter and led in to see Mr Butler, by request!

Before closing I might mention that tonight I was informed by Captain Roberts that my chief duty in life should be the practice of smiling on lonely officers. He personally was *"very lonely."*

Since moving to Hampstead my hours are: Mondays, Wednesdays and Fridays from 10 – 7.30.

DECEMBER 27th 1917

A line concerning my third Christmas in Hospital. Quite a jolly one too! Ward 34 looked beautiful in yellow and brown. The centre table being adorned with violets. At the last moment 48 hours leave was granted to all up patients so only some 15 officers remained in the ward for Christmas and they determined to enjoy themselves!

These valiant heroes had procured an alarming amount of mistletoe from dear knows where. Beaufort V.A.D. and myself felt quite safe and superior until the afternoon when half a dozen officers raided Sister's room where we were conversing. They were surely black and blue by the time they left us. I'm sure I never struggled and kicked so much in all my life – Beaufort acted likewise.

I thought I was attacking a Lt. Owen only to realise that I was fighting hard with a certain Captain Kepple Palmer. Then Mr Trail came on the scene. Later in the ward a comedian, Mr Mitchell, took advantage of the fact that I was heavily laden with trays – however, it being Christmas Day everyone had to be forgiven.

The wards were next visited and quite a jolly informal concert took place in the evening at which I visited. Before I continue I'd better confess that this year I certainly made up for last year's Christmas dinner (see entry). This year I'd no less than 4 Christmas dinners! In Streatham on the 24th, the officer's remnants on the 25th, with the staff on the 26th and at the comedy restaurant on the 26th! Publish it not to Rhondda!!

Today an unknown and beautiful naval 'hand' taxied me to the 'Elephant' and then paid my fare to Golders Green. My uniform must make an impression!

CHRISTMAS GREETINGS 1917.

SOMME, YPRE, ARRAS, MESSINES, ST. JULIEN, CAMBRAI.

All Best Wishes from

Eric.

XMAS & NEW YEAR
1917 — 1918

WITH BEST WISHES
FROM

Capt. P. Bennett
R.A.M.C.

❀ BEST WISHES ❀

FOR XMAS & NEW YEAR
FROM
Dorothy   Dec 1917.
B.R.C.S. AMBULANCE CONVOY.

o.a.s. Xmas 1917 – Whittle.

160.

JANUARY 14ᵗʰ 1918

It is said that more food is wasted in the 1ˢᵗ London General than any other hospital in London!

Upon entering the ward kitchen today the lady char informed me that "three food controllers" were on the prowl. She had the wind up properly but the officials never came near Ward 34, if ever they even entered the hospital.

I have been lent rather an interesting book. Mr Mitchell found it in a Boche dug out. It is an account of the U Boat "Deutschland".

My naval hand turned up once again yesterday. Great excitement! It seems that he is an old friend of our present Sister head who is taking Sister Atkins' holiday duty. Not long ago he taxied me to 'Elephant' and presented me with a ticket to Golders Green!

Mrs Flourie Steele.
Charlady, Ward 34.
1ˢᵗ London General Hospital.

JANUARY 29th 1918

Last night for the first time I felt myself personally at war! Leaving hospital about 8pm I had barely reached Brixton Road when the maroons echoed loudly in our ears and the tram car was immediately swamped with passengers. With considerable difficulty I extricated myself at the Oval only to find the Tube quite impossible. A seething mass of humanity swarmed around it on all sides. I crossed the road and took the next tram back to Hospital, where, after reporting to Matron I was led to the sister's sitting room on the second floor.

A number of sisters were gathered there and for the next two hours the guns entertained us right royally. Never have I known such crashes and when the barrage ceased the firing came from the heavens above where grim fighting took place. During an interval I counted ten objects flitting across the moon. Doubtless our own aeroplanes. A lull came shortly before eleven but I was not allowed home. Instead I was escorted to a tiny bedroom at the very top of the college. I jumped into bed and was just asleep when the guns sounded once more. Curiosity got the better of me and slipping on a coat I poked my head out of the door to hear a dry voice – oh, nurse – what's the good of anything? Why nothing ───────────

And a sleepy sister appeared on the scene. She and I had just descended the first flight of steps when an ear splitting crash deafened us entirely and whispers of "aerial torpedo" sounded on all sides. Then – the matron suddenly appeared – "Nurse! Go to the sitting room." – and once more I found myself there. However the firing soon ceased and I retired aloft to hear the all clear bugles.

Two dud shells landed on the hospital. The great crash was due to the collapse of John Bull's office at Covent Garden. Belsize Road, a mile from the Vicarage, was also badly strafed.

MARTIAL MISFITS

When the wounded give vent to their views
On the cut and the tint of their "blues".
And hankers a bit
For a nuttier kit
Denied by hard-hearted H.Qs.

Let them think of the poor V.A.D.
So chic and so dainty was she
With frillies galore
Ere the advent of war
Gripped her tight in its dogged decree.

Today when she's dressed for the street –
Her costume is stodgily neat,
A hat that's a fright
Hides her ringlets from sight,
And the length of her skirt is discreet.

But these "blues" and that V.A.D. dress
Though not an aesthetic success
Bring your war honoured tanks
Our national thanks,
Which are deeper, perhaps, than you guess.

APRIL 15th 1918

I copied this, "Wellington's Watchword" from the
calendar in Sister's sitting room, Ward 34.

*"Nothing in this life is really worth living for; one
can only go straight on and do one's duty."*

Myself, snapped by **Mr Brant**.

Capt Argols.

Capt. Duggen, Sister Lacey, Mr Jones,
Capt Argols and Padré Mackintosh.

164.

OCTOBER 29th 1918 – THE TERRACE – 10pm

Oct 23rd found me at the 1st London – The Ground Floor, Schools, proved my destination – a filthy hole – no other word describes it – as I went on duty at 2pm Proctor came off sick with the Plague (deadly "Spanish Flu").

The same day two sisters went off and the next morning Sister Cole, charge sister of the ward, died of pneumonia following flu. Knolls V.A.D. is still dangerously ill and half the hospital staff appears to be off duty.

On the ground floor I came across a repatriated one legged man, Pearson by name, who met Charles in Gilssen last month.

> Sec. Lt, RICHARD ROBERTSON TRAIL, R.G.A., Spec, Res.-For conspicuous gallantry and devotion to duty whilst acting as F.O.O. Although wounded and in great pain at the beginning of his tour of duty, he remained at his post for 18 hours, during which time he laid out wires and maintained communication in spite of heavy and continuous shelling.

I have now been shifted to Medical III where there is a ward of South Africans who fought against us in the Boer War. They are bringing one back to Zululand and are instructing me in their weird Dutch tongue.

THE HOSPITAL IS NOW IN QUARANTINE AND ENTIRELY ISOLATED!!!

Lights out!

> Charles Templeton was a Canadian Soldier and of Irish immigrant descent, related to the Denroche side. Taken prisoner he was eventually released as a Prisoner Of War, but made to find his own way home from Germany. He travelled as far as France where he contracted the deadly Influenza virus and died there.

OCTOBER 31st 1918

Some night tonight! Learner had a concert in the Y.M.C.A. I was on duty but ran round after tea to visit the Highwayman.

Arrived back in the ward to find Mr Bowes aspirating Fletcher, a South African. The needles did not fit the syringe and I was sent down to the theatre where I interviewed Sister – she strafed hard and delayed me a full two minutes enquiring as to why I had not returned the first box – surely any fool would realise that half of it was in use.

Next little Durgan – an original flu case – was discovered to have pus on the lung and was led to the theatre. Then five fresh flus walked in of varying temperatures – some life, this!

Last night funny little Le Margaund arrived up from the ground floor to say goodbye to me. He has promised me a bottle of Jersey Eau De Cologne. Hope it turns up!

NOVEMBER 2nd 1918

Eyken has just got in through the bottom of my window – was locked out and my ground floor cubicle proved useful. She spent some time on my bed while I recounted tales of the top floor schools.

Yesterday the sister, Reffles by name, went on night – a new one came on at 5 – she went on night today and I was left on alone with two wards of flu and pneumonia.

I frightened the life into one man to whom I was told to give oxygen if he looked at all blue. He looked awful bad at one time, so I produced the cylinder. I turned the thing on and there was a mighty bang! It roused the ward and oxygen was not necessary to rouse the patient!

Tonight a new flu came in with a temperature of close on 106. He was on leave from France. His recording thermometer so startled the new sister that a glass of hot milk was needed to revive her ladyship!

A Poem by JCBP

Vainly we strive to hear yon towering pinnacle of woe,
Vainly we beat our hands about its base.
Vainly we try to see the sun beyond
Better it were to climb the accursed tower,
And cast ourselves headlong, and so forget.

But stay, my friend, others have lived and died,
And never seen the dawn, come mount yon hill,
Look east, and see the sun break through the clouds.

Ah yes, but though the scene be bathed in light,
This very sun that shines so happily
Sharpens the shadows, darkens someone's room;
So woe is present in the brightest land,
And some must fall to make another great.

Fools that we are – we puppets of the gods,
Who strive so foolishly to gain our ends,
Who build our castles in the air, then God
Comes with His rod and knocks them down again.
Aye – fools we are, who curse our ill-starred fate,
And rile against the gods, and pray in vain
that good may come of some mad past mistake.
As if the gods cared for our sufferings here.
Ambition can't come true in Honesty.

Ambition's left for men who have no Faith
In Honour – come let's leave this sordid land,
Travel afar to some broad open space
And build our hut, and live in peace and rest
Out in the open flowery scented tracts
Out among nature, know its every way
And have no care – Look see infants
A vast great panorama through the mist.
Blue mountains, black dark shady woods and streams
Dashing their merry music to the rock below
And gathering at the base gush on in mad
And merry wantoness joy - oh come with me
Far from these crowded towns and people bare
And live the open free wild eye and die
Happy, unknown in some far distant land.

Life is a book where many things we see –
God as its author and His puppets we –
At the author's wish our wills submissive bend –
Until He's done with us – and then He writes "the End."

SERGEANT: "Private Blobbs, report yourself at the Orderly Room at once for leavin' the ranks without permission!"

Pte. A. Crossley
N. Staff
Regt
(formerly in the
Yorks Regt)

ARMISTICE SIGNED.

HOSTILITIES CEASED AT 11AM WHEN MAROONS PROCLAIMED THE NEWS IN THE LONDON AREA.

Never shall I forget this day! Monday November 11th. News reached the Hospital early in the morning that hostilities would cease at 11am. As the maroons sounded, Blasson and myself solemnly shook hands mid hectic confusion on the corridor where we were nursing sick sisters.

From the windows we could see a crowd of blues flying off duty(!) without a pass – that same afternoon Fenner, Blasson and I made for town – an Australian Tommy hoisted us on to a crowded tram car with these words: *"If it weren't for you girls we shouldn't have won this war today!"*

From Victoria we struggled through the throng to Buckingham Palace where we stood for an hour while an excited multitude proclaimed:

"WE WANT GEORGE."
"WE WANT GEORGE."

They were rewarded by seeing him drive off to St. Pauls.

I'm so sleepy and in bed – must continue.............. tomorrow!

ODE ON DEPARTURE OF THE V.A.D.s

As you leave for the war with your cross on your breast,
With your bright hypodermic and medicine chest,
With your cap and your uniform neat as can be,
And a manner professional wondrous to see;
Will you answer a question - come bend your proud head,
It's simply, my dear, can you make up a bed?

As the ward entertainer, you carry a punch,
You're there in the pinches and play the right hunch,
You know all the ragtimes, you sing like an Eames,
You can beat all the best at their favourite games;
You can fascinate man with your silvery laugh,
But - candidly now - can you give him a bath?

You can understand french when one murmur's "cherie",
And your instincts will tell you just when to say "oui",
There's never a dialect 'mongst the Allies,
Excepting the Russian, to which you're not wise;
But the doctors, prosaic old things that they are,
Can you understand them when they ask "T.P.R."?

The poor Tommy's heart, heavy with pain,
At the sound of your steps starts its beating again,
And the touch of your finger, as light as a leaf,
Makes squabs and champagne out of old Bully Beef;
You can make Tommy gasp, blush, catch his breath,
But – what would you do were he bleeding to death?

We may have thought these things in June 'seventeen,
Now we blush at the thought of what scoffers we've been,
You are amiable, beautiful, capable, kind,
And your talents convince the most sceptical mind.
Of all the war's horrors - the greatest of these,
Is the thought that we're losing you - dear V.A.D.s!

POSTSCRIPT

John Brunsdon MBE

After the war Grace Pulvertaft left the V.A.D. and enrolled at RADA (The Royal Academy of Dramatic Art). There she acquired skills in drama, elocution and speech therapy. Subsequently she had a successful career teaching in a number of girls schools up until her marriage to Cpt Fred Brunsdon.

Fred had volunteered at the start of war enlisting in the Artists Rifles, later transferring to the Hertfordshire Reg. He was in the trenches, contracted Peritonitis and barely made it back to England. Recovered, he was appointed Commandant of a P.O.W. camp when prisoners went out to tidy up ruined towns. He was mentioned in despatches to do with the unloading of a burning munitions train. Fred was an ex-Kilburn grammar school lad. He had started at the Westminster Bank pre war but had to start again after, at the bottom, as he had 'volunteered'!

He rose through the office ranks reaching Chief Clerk at Loughton branch, soon to be with Grace in the 2nd World War as air raid wardens during The Blitz as well. He was appointed manager at Westerham branch during the Flying Bomb (V.1.) period. As chairman of the local British Legion he invited Winston Churchill to meet the members at the club – including his daughter driver Mary (Soames). Fred retired as manager from the Reigate branch.

At each of the job location changes Grace, in addition to bringing up sons David and John, would join the Women's Institute invariably serving as President before having to move on. She instilled an interest in drama and play-reading in the members. A performance of 'A Midsummer Nights Dream' on the edge of Epping Forest was memorable. Occasionally she would help, at no charge, a W.I. member's relative who might have a speech difficulty.

As a child I recall her doing the house work at the same time reciting William Blake's lyrical poems. Both parents, but Grace in particular, emphasised the importance of education and gave David and myself every encouragement. Both of us were educated at St. Lawrence Ramsgate at considerable financial self sacrifice. David was gifted and qualified as a Doctor at Guys Hospital at an early age. Serving first with the RAF, he decided to emigrate to Canada. He had already specialised in Pathology and finished as Director of the Department at Toronto Hospital. I qualified as a Veterinary Surgeon at London practicing in Glastonbury, Somerset where I also served as mayor 3 times.

Grace and Fred retired to April Cottage Littlehempston, Devon. Both enjoyed gardening and visits from grandchildren. Fred served on the Totnes Rural District Council, eventually as chairman with Grace at his side to support him at functions. They never owned a car. Money was spent on other things instead; and are gratefully remembered in Littlehempston churchyard.

Cpt Fred Brunsdon.

Grace Pulvertaft.

LEST WE FORGET

PTE. E. CROSSLEY,
N. STAFFS. REGT.
(Formerly of the Yorks.
Regt.)